Title: HTML: The Intuitive Guide
Edition: I
Release: March 12, 2018
Genre: Software Education
Publisher: Learning Curve Books
Imprint: Independently published
ISBN: 9781980538301
Author: Greg Sidelnikov
Contact: greg.sidelnikov@gmail.com

The primary purpose of Learning Curve Book publishing company is to provide *effective education* for our readers. We hope you enjoy learning from this edition of *HTML: The Intuitive Guide*. For questions and comments about the book you may contact the author or send an email directly to our office at the email address mentioned below.

Special Offers & Discounts Available

Schools, libraries and educational organizations may qualify for special prices. Get in touch with our distribution department at **hello@learningcurvebook.net**

Learning Curve Books, LLC.

©2018

Contents

0.1 Introduction

0.2 Who Is This Book For?

This book is an introduction to the HTML language. Careful choices were made in order to provide *maximum insight* into HTML language for beginners coming to the world of web design and development *for the first time*. My hope is that this book accomplishes this task.

0.3 Book Format

A great deal of time was taken to deliver continuity of content that makes the entire passage of this book readable from cover to cover *gradually* illuminating the subjects that build knowledge on sections covered in prior chapters.

But this book can also be used as a *reference* where each chapter focuses on one side of web design with HTML language that you may need to look up at a particular time *on demand*.

In my personal experience as a web designer and software developer over the last decade – looking back – it became clear to me that even though HTML is an extensive language with seemingly never-ending *tags*, *attributes*, *events* and *CSS properties*, in practical reality you need to gain good understanding only of a handful techniques for developing professional websites and applications.

Besides, *knowing too much* of HTML in relation to CSS and JavaScript may backfire on you since not all features are supported in the same way by all browsers (*Chrome*, *Firefox*, *Internet Explorer*, *Safari*, *Opera*, etc.) as recommended by the W3C(https://www.w3.org/html/).

Instead of providing complete documentation of the HTML language this book has a humble goal of focusing on following issues:

1. **Focus on Practical Features.** Several years of experience with the HTML language were poured out and converged into chapters of this book dealing with issues that actually matter in practice. These are the subjects that you would *repetitively* come across regardless of your experience level with HTML.

2. **Visual Diagrams.** HTML is a visual language. By writing HTML code, you co-dependently construct visual appearance of your website. A large amount of time was spent on crafting custom diagrams to describe what HTML elements look like on a web page. This helps if you're reading the book in your spare time riding a bus on your way to work. Perhaps you simply don't have time to actually open the browser just to see what a single HTML element looks like while reading the book.

3. **Cascading Style Sheets.** HTML is part of the "trinity" of languages that together help you create beautiful websites and web applications: HTML, CSS and JavaScript. It would be a disservice to the beginner HTML developer to not talk about CSS (*Cascading Style Sheets*) at all because the two are so closely related. Instead of creating a pure HTML book, we decided that describing how HTML layouts are affected by CSS would only add value to this book.

4. **JavaScript.** The JavaScript language is an important element of web development. It may have been acceptable to not talk about it at all in the early 90's, when HTML was a young language. But this cannot be said with the same degree of certainty today. JavaScript provides a way to customize dynamic functionality of your website. In 2018, the year this book was written, JavaScript has long earned reputation of being more than just a scripting language. Entire front-end for web applications is usually created with the help of JavaScript. HTML structure is designed around DOM (*Document Object Model,*) and JavaScript is the language that was originally designed to work with the DOM. For these reasons it was decided that JavaScript code should make casual appearance throughout the book. Toward the ending chapters we will also demonstrate several examples of simple web applications such as *Clock* and *Calculator* the dynamic features of which (tracking which buttons were clicked, or animating the clock's hand) would not be possible without JavaScript.

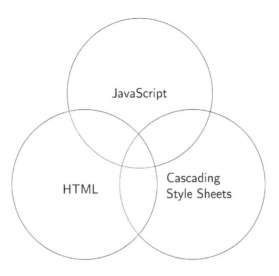

Figure 1: HTML, CSS and JavaScript form The Holy Trinity of modern Web Design and Development. No matter what type of HTML you will write, there is always some overlap between the three. If you're learning one – you're learning at least part of the other two.

In this book, chapters were carefully chosen to help the new-comers get up to speed on their journey to becoming a professional Web Designer or Web Application Developer.

It is assumed that the reader will spend additional time to do the research on their own. However, this is a fairly reasonable assumption to make for any technical book.

The contents of this book were designed to help with the learning process. Hopefully it will become an insightful and helpful volume in your home library of software books.

By focusing only on the most important parts of HTML language, we hope to have created a good reference to help the reader become a better web designer, and we truly hope this book accomplishes this task.

Well I think this is enough background for now and we're getting ready to start learning HTML!

But before we move forward, let's take a look at how you can preview your website files in your browser. After that we will deep-dive into construction of websites and applications with HTML.

0.4 Where Do I Enter HTML Code?

You are probably an owner of a PC running Windows Operating System, or Mac running OSX. Luckily for us, HTML can be written in any standard text editor on the Operating System of your choice.

There are several IDEs (Integrated Development Environments) that help speed up development time. These are usually the advanced text editors designed specifically for writing code. But what if you don't want to spend money on an HTML editor? No problem. You can start by experimenting with HTML using your standard text editors that already come free and pre-installed with your Operating System.

0.4.1 Windows PC

If you are on a Windows based PC, you can type HTML into Notepad.exe, the standard text editor that comes pre-installed with Windows.

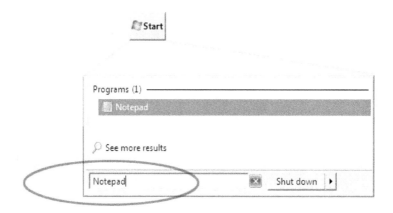

Figure 2: Click on the "Start" button in Windows, type "Notepad" where it says "Search Programs and Files" and hit Enter.

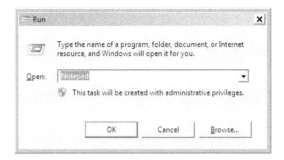

Figure 3: Alternatively, you can find Notepad by holding down the "Windows Key" and pressing "R" key at the same time. Type "Notepad" in the box that opens and hit "Enter" key.

Do one of the steps above and after hitting Enter key a fresh copy of Notepad editor should open!

There are other ways to access Notepad on Windows, and you may as well create an icon on your Desktop to make repetitive access more convenient in the future.

Here is some HTML code for a very simple page. It is typed directly into Notepad, as shown in the following diagram:

```
Untitled - Notepad                                               _ □ ×
File  Edit  Format  View  Help
<html>
    <head>
        <title>Hello, welcome to my website!</title>
    </head>
    <body>
        <!-- An HTML comment //-->
        <div id = "container">
            <h1>Lunar Pull</h1>
            <p>The greatest site.</p>
            <p>Is the first site.</p>
            <p>You ever make.</p>
        </div>
    </body>
</html>
```

Figure 4: An example of a very simple website typed into Notepad on Windows Operating System. Just a few lines of HTML code can be used to construct a page with a header and basic text. We'll go in much greater detail to inspect commonly used HTML tags throughout the rest of this book.

To save your file in HTML format, you must change file format in Window's "save file" Dialog Box after you click File > Save on the Notepad menu bar:

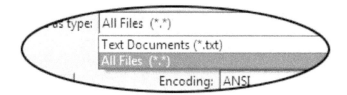

Figure 5: After clicking "Save" this dialog shows up. It is important to change default file type to `All Files(*.*)"` instead of `Text Documents (.txt)`

When saving your HTML files, you must save them using the `.html` file extension, and not the default `.txt` reserved for plain text files. Otherwise, your browser will not recognize it as an HTML file and will not be able to render your webpage in the view, but display it as plain text.

The HTML format is still technically a text file. But the browser will *interpret* it as an HTML page only if its saved with `.html` extension.

The homepage file is usually saved as `index.html`. Other pages on your site can be saved separately, for example: `contact.html`, `about.html`, etc.

0.4.2   Mac

Likewise, you can use textEdit, the built-in text editor on the Mac OSX. In order to access it, locate the small magnifying glass in the upper right corner of the screen, and start typing "textEdit". The OSX should automatically find the application before you finish typing the whole name:

Figure 6: Click on magnifying glass and type "textEdit"

Figure 7: Locate textEdit by typing it into the box that shows up.

Finally, once textEdit is opened, you can type your HTML into it in the same way as you would in Notepad on Windows:

7

```
<html>
  <head>
    <title>Hello, welcome to my website!</title>
  </head>
  <body>
    <!-- An HTML comment //-->
    <div id = "container">
      <h1>Lunar Pull</h1>
      <p>The greatest site.</p>
    <p>Is the first site.</p>
    <p>You ever make.</p>
    </div>
  </body>
</html>
```

Figure 8: Typing HTML code into textEdit on a Mac.

A good editor on a Mac called `TextWrangler` can be used before moving on to advanced IDE's. It's compact, allows working on multiple files at the same time, and has support for automatically uploading your files to your web host (the online web server hosting your files from a "www" address.)

Basic editors are great for learning. But if you are looking to grow in your web development career, I recommend finding a good IDE. When working professionally, it is rare for developers to use just the basic text editors.

0.5 Integrated Development Environment

Numerous advanced editors called IDEs (short for *Integrated Development Environment*) exist that will make your life as a web developer easier. With features that make accomplishing common or repetitive tasks more efficiently, they often help streamline the process of building a website or web application.

Using an IDE is optional and the best ones are usually not free. However

8

if I had to recommend absolutely the best IDE for HTML and JavaScript development, it would have to be JetBrain's *WebStorm*. These IDEs provide useful features such as, ability to upload your site to your domain name simply by saving the file. (Otherwise, you should use an "FTP" program to upload all web files *manually* to your web host.) IDEs provide many other features that just get a lot of rudimentary work out of the way so you can focus on coding.

0.6   Viewing Your Website In a Web Browser

You don't have to upload your HTML website to a web host at a "www" location in order to preview it in your browser. You can preview it locally in "offline" mode directly from your hard drive.

To view your HTML file in a browser, save it somewhere on your hard drive. Open your browser (Let's say *Chrome*) side by side with your Windows Explorer (or "Finder" on a Mac.) Locate the HTML file you created containing your website code (*index.html* for example) and then *drag and drop it directly into the browser.*

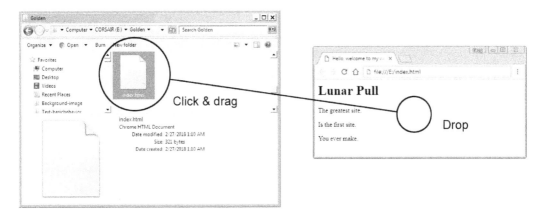

Figure 9: Drag and drop your HTML file into your browser to preview it.

Now that we got the basics out of the way we're ready to start learning HTML language!

9

The rest of this book will guide you through descriptions of common HTML tags. We will create and gain control over size, position and special properties of common HTML elements. They are the blocks on the screen that help us construct entire websites and common User Interface designs.

Together with your patience and creativity this book will guide you toward creating beautiful websites. You can also take this knowledge to another level and learn how to build layouts for *web applications*.

This book provides a solid foundation to get started.

1 Chapter I – Primal HTML

In the beginning of the 90's HTML became the standard language for creating websites. In those times, the language was pretty basic with just a number of HTML tags defining a few visual elements for creating simple page design similar to that of a newspaper.

Although HTML has not undergone many changes to its core specification since its original conception, it is often the starting point language for those who are new to the world of web development.

If web development is a brick house where a large majority of visual and dynamic content is provided by Cascading Style Sheets (CSS) and JavaScript respectively, then HTML is the cement laid in between.

Today, HTML is used to provide structure to websites, but more importantly to web applications that display text, graphics and multimedia content. You may have picked this book up because you were looking to become a graphic designer and learn how to make websites.

Or perhaps you saw a web application and wanted to learn how create one of your own. Although building complex web applications requires advanced knowledge of languages such as JavaScript, at the fundamental level the structural layout of any website or application is created in HTML which stands for Hypertext Markup Language.

1.1 Getting Started

Let's begin our journey by learning the basics. In HTML, we use tags to define structure. Most of your HTML code will consist of tags. When viewed in browser a tag becomes an HTML element. Elements are tags represented visually on the screen. Throughout this book the word tag and element will be used interchangeably based on context. But what is an HTML tag exactly?

1.2   Anatomy of an HTML Tag

A tag is the single building block of your HTML document. They often begin with an angular bracket that looks like < and end with a closing bracket >. Whatever goes in between is referred to as the tag's name. Each tag has a unique purpose.

Let's take a look at some examples:

```
1       <html> is  used  for  enclosing  your  entire  HTML  document.
2       <head> includes  non-content  information,  such  as
            external  scripts,  written  in  JavaScript,  CSS  and  so
            on.
3       <script> Include  a  script  file,  usually  written  in
            JavaScript.
4       <title> The  browser  title  of  your  webpage.
5       <body> Content  of  your  entire  webpage.
6       <p> A  paragraph  of  text.
7       <h1> Large  header  text.
```

These are just a few tags out of hundreds that you can use to define structure of your web page. To display anything meaningful within these tags, however, tags listed above are usually paired with a closing tag with the same name.

1.3   Pairing HTML Tags

A large majority of HTML tags are used in pair with their closing equivalent. Whatever goes in between the opening and closing tag is known as that tag's content.

For example:

```
1       <body> Entire  body  of  our  website
2       will  be  placed  here  </body>
3
4       <h1>A  large  header  title</h1>
5
6       <p> I  am  just  a  paragraph  of  text. You  can
7       write  any  text  here.  </p>
```

1.4 Closing Tags In Correct Order

It's important to close tags around its content in the same order they were opened. Otherwise you risk confusing the browser's HTML code processor if tags were supplied in mangled order. Try to avoid these common errors:

<body> Entire body of our website will be placed here

In this example the <body> tag was opened, but it was never closed. Here HTML is forgiving enough to close the tag on its own when your page is actually viewed in the browser. It will still appear correctly. Remember, HTML was invented to deal with dynamic content even before a web page is fully loaded into the browser. That means that it is essential for web browsers to handle cases where HTML cuts off at some obscure place. However, this doesn't qualify it as correct HTML code or give us a good excuse not to properly close HTML tags.

<p>I am an example of <b>bold text in a single paragraph.</p
 >

Here we have forgotten to close <b> tag, which stands for bold text. The browser will still apply the bold formatting to the remainder of the sentence, but it's not what we want. Correct version is displayed below:

<p>I am an example of <b>bold text</b> in a single paragraph
 .</p>

Here the <b> tag is closed at a correct place, making the phrase "bold text" appear in bold letters when viewed from your browser.

We have just created some extremely basic examples demonstrating how HTML is used to format text. In just a moment we will see what kind of result this HTML code produces when it's viewed in the browser. Throughout this book we will use Google Chrome for displaying results of our HTML experiments!

And to move forward with that, let's take a look at a slightly more complex example where we will use tag nesting.

1.5 Nested Tags

Every HTML page usually contains a number of nested tags. They help us *semantically* divide our HTML document into sections. Some tags will contain plain text content as shown in the previous example. While other tags like `<div>` use nesting to divide the web page into sub-sections to create your visual layout structure. Below you will see a trivial nesting example.

```
1   <div>
2     <div>
3       <div>
4         <h1>A list of my items</h1>
5         <h2>Slightly smaller sub-header text.</h2>
6         <p><b>Figure 1.</b> My amazing list of items. <span>
              Consisting of random text.</span></p>
7         <ul>
8           <li>First item on my list</li>
9           <li>Second item on my list</li>
10          <li>Third item on my list</li>
11        </ul>
12      </div>
13    </div>
14  </div>
```

Note that all tags close in the same oder they were opened. The `<div>` tags here are used only as an example. They make no difference on the layout of your page in this case, because they gracefully fold into one another. We'll discover how this actually works later in the book when we talk about position of elements on the screen.

Go ahead, save this HTML in a file (*nested.html* for example) and drag and drop it into your Chrome browser.

And here are the results:

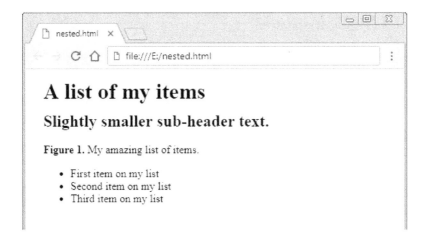

Figure 10: Nested tags can be used to create general structure for displaying content. Beside the nested `<div>` tags, that were used only as an example – and have no visual effect – in this instance I used two HTML tags we haven't seen yet: `<ul>` and `<li>`. These tags form an "unordered list", a bulletin point list where instead of numbers a leading dot character appears to indicate a unique item on the list. Note also that text inside `<h1></h1>` tags appears in much larger font. The `<h1>` tag, which stands for header, is used just for that purpose. There are also `<h2>`, `<h3>`, `<h4>`, `<h5>` and `<h6>` tags used for sub-header text. The `<h6>` header is the smallest of them all.

Some of the tags transform into a particular type of formatting when applied to your text content. In general however, you will find yourself using `<div>` tags a lot to accomplish the task of building out overall structure of a webpage or user interface for your web application.

In the HTML source code that produces results shown in Figure 1. we have a series of `<div>` elements which stands for "division". Later when we get to CSS styling chapters we will see how `<div>` elements can be modified to appear anywhere on the screen, rather than in sequential order one below the other. Also, you will learn how to change background color and many other properties of a `<div>` element with CSS.

1.6 HTML Comments

HTML comments are created using `<!--` and `//-->` bracket pair. Anything that goes in between these two brackets will not be processed by internal HTML engine or appear on the screen. It will not become part of your page structure. Instead, comments simply provide helpful description of the code that follows.

In a real-world setting, if you happen to design websites for a living, you are likely to work with other HTML programmers or web developers. Using comments helps to evangelize the rest of your team so they get an idea of what you were thinking about when you were writing your code.

```
1  <h1>Top 10 Albums of All Time</h1>
2
3  <!-- A list of top music albums of all time //-->
4  <table>
5    <tr>
6      <td>Position</td>
7      <td>Album</td>
8      <td>Artist</td>
9    </tr>
10 </table>
```

This line of code here:

```
1  <!-- A list of top music albums of all time //-->
```

It represents an HTML comment. None of the content in it is actually rendered in the browser. The message is usually a side note for the web developers alone.

1.6.1 Multi-line Comments

An HTML comment can span across multiple lines.

```
1  <h1>Top 10 Albums of All Time</h1>
2
3  <!-- A multi-line comment can be used to temporarily disable
       HTML
```

```
 4  <table>
 5    <tr>
 6      <td>Position</td>
 7      <td>Album</td>
 8      <td>Artist</td>
 9    </tr>
10  </table> //-->
```

Now the entire `<table>` is enclosed by comment brackets and will not be rendered in the browser view but it will still be kept in the document. And if you want to enable it later, simply uncomment it again.

Sometimes comments are used in a clever way to temporarily disable a block of code *without* actually removing it from the document.

1.7 Relative, Absolute, Blocking And Inline Elements

In HTML there are two primary ways of determining positioning of an element: "relative" and "absolute." A large number of tags in HTML have their position set to "relative" or "unset" by default. This is why all of the tags in the examples up to this point in the book appeared one after the other order when rendered in browser.

A `<div>` or any other element can also be situated at what HTML refers to as an "absolute" position. In HTML an "absolute" position of an element is determined by two additional properties called "top" and "left" whose values are specified in pixels. These values represent how far to the left and bottom your element is located, relative to the position of its parent element. This means you have control over exactly where the element will appear on your page, or at least within its parent.

Quick Note. In HTML nested tags have a parent / child relationship. Just like in real life, children come from parents. And some of the children can have their own children. This means that some children elements are also parents to the tags nested within them.

In addition, content within any of these types of elements can be set up to either "block" all other elements, or appear "inline" with them. You'll see how this works in a later chapter of this book on page structure. Here we speak about this only to give you an idea that you have more control over element placement which we will explore in greater detail in this book.

1.8   When Code Becomes Design

But what about this example where tags are nested or written one after the other? Simply nesting an element does not always automatically drop it to the next line of text. Not all HTML tags are expected to behave in exactly the same way based on their type. Even when they enclose the same type of content.

For this reason, much of your mastery of HTML language will come from practice. In my experience people who love to write HTML code also often develop graphic design skills.

Because HTML code and the visual design of your page's layout are correlated, many HTML programmers acquire this type of knowledge intuitively as they experiment and write more HTML code. Juggle around tags in your HTML document to see how they affect the layout on the screen when you save your document and refresh it in your browser to see the changes.

1.9   Default Style

In HTML many tags are assigned a "default" CSS style even if you didn't specify it yourself.

For example, using two `<span>` tags in a row, will not generate a line break. But two `<div>` tags in a row will. This is simply because span tag's default CSS "display" style is set to "inline-block", which perpetuates any text added after it just to the end of the previous tag. But `<div>` tag's default "display" property style is "block", which will drop content added to your HTML document immediately after the `<div>` tag right below it, based on the height of that `<div>` element.

You'll learn to intuitively understand what these default styles do for different types of tags as you continue experimenting.

Notice also that the `<b>` tag (bold text) around "Figure 1" is nested within the `<p>` tag. One `<ul>` container tag and three `<li>` tags were used to create an unordered list in this example. The `<b>` tag's default "display" style is "inline-block", and so for this reason the bold text "Figure 1" neatly falls into the integrity of the rest of the sentence in that paragraph.

1.10   Overnesting

In HTML, we can create ordered and unordered lists. An unordered list will use a small character such as a filled or empty dot. An ordered list will automatically assign a digit to the list's item based on its order.

This is just one out of the dozens of tags you will use to construct your layout.

Although not entirely necessary, in a real-world scenario you probably want to avoid long nesting chains, unless completely necessary. In this example we have a series of empty `<div>` tags shown only as an example of how nesting works.

Best Practice. When creating your layout try to avoid deep nesting, if possible. While this will not affect performance of your website it might affect its readability. It is also a lot easier to maintain clean code in the long run, in case you want to update it with new functionality or adjust an existing feature. Just a few levels of nesting is enough. Try to aim at 3 to 5 levels per unique User Interface element for best readability.

Websites like blogs and many others consist of several nesting levels. However, some user Interface designs require that you go beyond that. This is commonly true of building web applications. Just take a look at the source code of Twitter or Facebook, if you're not yet convinced.

More than often, though, deep nesting is an after effect of bad design.

In this book we will continue to keep things as simple as possible. Toward the end we will build a simple web application just to demonstrate that HTML is not limited to creating simple websites. An example of a fully functional calculator application will put everything we talked about in the book together. We're a bit far from that point right now. Until then, let's continue our journey and exploration of primal HTML.

1.11   Self-Closing Tags

Self-closing tags do not require to be paired.

Most common examples of single self-closing tags are `<br/>` and `<hr/>` and a few others. They do not need to be paired with a second closing tag. This is because self-closing tags assume not to bear any content within them. Their function is usually decorative. `<br/>` tag is the Break tag which is often used as paragraph modifier. Some HTML programmers mistakenly use it for creating spacing between elements. Because it's so easy to copy and paste a bunch of `<br/>` tags into your code!

```
1  <hr/> Creates a wide horizontal line between paragraphs or
       content
2  <br/> Create a line break
3  <p>This is a paragraph</p>
4  <br/>
5  <br/>
6  <br/>
7  <p>Another paragraph 3 line breaks down</p>
```

1.12   Tags or Elements?

Tags and Elements are often used interchangeably in conversation between graphic designers. But are they really one and the same? An HTML element is usually the visual representation of a pair of tags. Tags *become* elements when they are rendered on the screen in your browser.

Here you can see how an element is an encompassing block consisting of two tags: an opening `<p>` tag pairsed with its closing `</p>` equivalent to signify a paragraph of text.

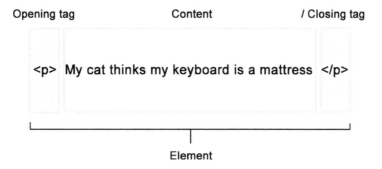

Figure 11: How tags construct elements.

But what about self-closing tag like `</br>` and `</hr>` for example?

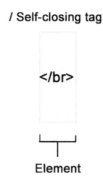

Figure 12: A self-closing tag.

It is open to interpretation whether you want to call them self-closing tags or elements. But generally, think of elements as a higher-order tags. Sometimes you'll hear programmers refer to the `<img />` tag – the one responsible for displaying images in your HTML document – as "image element" or "image tag." The same goes for most other tags.

1.13 Using HTML Tags For Their Intended Purpose

With time you will learn how to use each HTML tag for its intended purpose. However, with enough experience some HTML developers start to use

Unordered Lists for the purpose of creating a navigation system, for example. They just strip away the default CSS formatting.

This is often acceptable, and in fact desired, because search engines such as Google treat site navigation *semantically* which usually helps your website appear as more organized and sometimes improve search engine ranking.

In most cases, try not to follow short cuts if you doubt that there isn't a better way. There is a good chance that there exists a tag specifically dedicated for solving a particular problem.

And if that isn't the case, often CSS is used for applying modifications to HTML tags. How they are used together with HTML is a whole different story. Try to keep integrity of sticking to standard practice throughout your code as much as possible.

Best Practice. Use tags for their intended purpose. For example, avoid using `<br/>` tag simply to create more space between text or images. For that purpose, use `padding` and `margin` in external CSS script or directly within an attribute of the HTML tag in question.

We'll discuss padding and margin properties later in the book. We're not quite there yet. We must first explore attributes and properties and this is the next subject of this book.

1.14 Tag Attributes and Properties

Up to this point we learned how to create basic webpage structure with common nesting techniques. We also learned to create paragraphs of text and make lists.

In order to make HTML tags display more intriguing content or provide additional functionality to HTML elements we can use **attributes** and **properties**.

HTML tag *attributes* require values. Whereas *properties* are usually stand-alone keywords that enable or disable certain feature of that tag. For example a property can determine if a check box is checked by default on page load.

Here, `checked` is a property that was added to the input tag:

```
<input type = "checkbox" checked />
```

And here is another example. This time, the property `disabled` added to a text input field will gray it out, and make changing the value of that input field impossible:

```
<input type = "text" disabled />
```

In the long past HTML elements used to support now deprecated attributes such as color. For example, adding color attribute to a paragraph tag, would paint the text red:

```
<p color = "red">This paragraph used to appear in red
   letters</p>
```

Don't get me wrong. If you use this code and display it in Chrome browser, nothing will change. The attribute color is long deprecated.

I just want to demonstrate that we can use attributes to extend functionality of HTML tags. Attributes usually have a name and a value. In example above name was color and value was a text string "red". And valueless attributes are called properties.

```
<input type = "radio" name = "animal" default /> Cats
<input type = "radio" name = "animal"/> Dogs
<input type = "radio" name = "animal"/> Donkeys
```

Note that `default` here is a property. By its mere presence on this tag it indicates that the radio button for "Cats" will be selected as the default choice when page loads.

Note. A string is a line of text. When we get to JavaScript in later chapters, we will see how JavaScript variables also have a name and a value. This is common in web development. Whenever we need a value in text format, these values are often referred to as strings. You will know them by the fact that they are often wrapped in single or double quotes.

Let's consider this other example that will actually color text inside the `<p>` tag in red color:

```
<p style = "color:_red">This paragraph will appear in red.</
   p>
```

Here we used the **style** attribute to add CSS to our HTML tag. But the value
"color: red" is not written in HTML language. Here, instead of equal sign we
use a colon instead. Whatever is specified using style attribute will always be
written in CSS language. It has a different syntax than HTML.

This example shows how easy it is to combine HTML and CSS together in one
tag. And here is another example, this time using single quote strings. But
there is no difference:

```
<p style = 'color: red'>This paragraph will appear in red.</
   p>
```

HTML, CSS and JavaScript are nearly inseparable languages that form the
holy trinity of web development as a whole. CSS provides the style. And
JavaScript provides custom, dynamic functionality to your HTML layout making building interactive User Interfaces easier and more fun.

Because this is primarily an HTML book we won't be diving into CSS or
JavaScript until later chapters. But to avoid talking about either one of the
two would be a disservice to the reader.

1.15   Event Attributes

At this point in the book what's important to understand is that HTML tags
are often accompanied by attributes. Some attributes provide access to CSS.
While others act as events written in JavaScript language. For example, the
following paragraph tag will create a popup alert when clicked.

```
<p onclick = "alert('I_am_an_alert_box!')">Click me!</p>
```

Clicking on this paragraph will display a modal Alert box in Chrome browser:

There is a multitude of events you can use in your HTML tags. They all will
be covered at an appropriate place in the book as we make progress.

All this is only touching the tip of the iceberg! Of course it is possible to write
entire programs in JavaScript and integrate them with your HTML layout,

Figure 13: An alert box triggered by onclick event on an HTML paragraph tag.

all within a single HTML document (for example in a homepage file called `index.html`). But I don't want to go farther than this at this point in the book. Until then, we have a few other things to cover.

1.16   HTML Document Structure

As you continue building out your page structure you will notice that overall most pages will follow the same pattern where `<head>` and `<body>` will be placed inside `<html>` tag.

Each tag with a unique name exists to serve its primary purpose. For example `<html>` tag will encompass your entire HTML document. The `<head>` tag is used to store non-content information such as meta tags, language, character encoding, copyright and general information about the site.

HTML Document Structure. Before we provide details for all kinds of different HTML elements later in the book it's good to get a bird's eye view of the full picture. Below is a common structure of an HTML page:

```
1  <!DOCTYPE html>
2  <html>
3    <head>
4      <title>Basic HTML Document</title>
5      <meta name = "description"
6          content = "My wonderful website, including cat
               pictures, and a few of my own experiments with the
               artistic elements of photography.">
```

```
 7        <meta name = "keywords"
 8            content = "cats ,photos ,experiments">
 9      <head>
10      <body>
11        <ul>
12          <li>First item on my list</li>
13          <li>Second item on my list</li>
14          <li>Third item on my list</li>
15        </ul>
16      </body>
17    </html>
```

Instead of aimlessly trying to create HTML elements that do nothing in particular, we are now looking at a legitimate HTML document structure. All pages you will create from now on will have at least this skeletal design!

Notice here the addition of two `<meta>` tags. A meta tag does not affect visual layout of your page. The same goes for any tag located within the head tags in your HTML document. They're here for descriptive purpose alone. Or for adding external scripts (more on this later.) In other words these meta tags are here only to suggest some information about the content of your website.

These meta tags require both attributes: name and content. In name, you will specify the type of the meta tag. And in description, you will specify the value of the meta tag related to its name.

Meta tags are present on almost all web pages that exist on the Internet. They serve this simple purpose:

- **description** meta tags are read by Google search engine to provide information shown along with your website when it appears as a search result, just below the website title. They briefly outline the purpose of your website.

- **keyword** meta tags are also used by search engines. For its value, use targeted keywords that describe your website with as much precision as possible. Each keyword should be separated by a comma or space.

Be as specific as possible. What you enter in meta tags may (or may not)

26

affect how your website ranks on Google. This technique used to be much more effective among those who wanted to "search-engine optimize" their website for better ranking. And although modern search engine algorithms give meta tags less attention when trying to determine relevancy of a website, it is still important to be as descriptive as possible when using them.

1.17 DOCTYPE

While we will not cover all of the meta tags and various details of constructing a complete site header in HTML (primarily because they have no practical effect on either success of your website with search engines, or achieving useful layout or design function,) DOCTYPE deserves a little of our attention.

`<!DOCTYPE html>` directive determines HTML version of the document. Nowadays this is the most common directive. Although there are a few other alternatives, but we're not concerned with them right now. For now, let's assume that all HTML pages will start with `<!DOCTYPE html>`.

We've also used `<head>`, `<title>` and `<body>` tags to define a basic HTML document structure. You will find this common pattern in just about every site. This pattern is the standard way of starting any webpage, and it has not changed since the 90's.

Just as an example we've also used the now familiar HTML tags used for creating Unordered Lists: `<ul>` and `<li>`. It will create a list of items as shown in the screen shot below when this HTML code is displayed in Chrome browser:

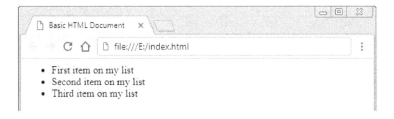

Figure 14: Notice "Basic HTML Document" appears as name of the tab.

1.18 Specifying Website Title

By specifying text between `<title>`here`</title>` tags we tell the browser what to display in the tab when our website is viewed online. Note that the title tag should be nested under head tag.

1.19 Inline, Internal & External Code

In one of our previous examples we demonstrated how JavaScript can be called directly from an HTML attribute. As your website grows in size you will find yourself adding a lot more CSS and possibly JavaScript code. It's not uncommon for a medium size web application to draw a distinction between HTML, CSS and JavaScript by providing a place to separate one language from the other.

`Inline` Writing CSS or JavaScript directly into an HTML style attribute or various event attributes.

`Internal` To associate CSS or JavaScript code internally right within your HTML code you can place CSS code inside stand-alone `<style>` tags. And JavaScript inside stand-alone `<script>` tags. This all can be done within the same index.html file together with your main HTML code.

`External` In order to prevent large convoluted files HTML offers ability to store CSS and JavaScript files externally in separate files apart from the main `index.html` file. For example all of your CSS code could go inside "style.css" and JavaScript code could be stored in `script.js`. Then, these files are "included" or "added" using `<link>` (for CSS) or `<script>` tags respectively.

Source Code Examples

Let's expand on previous source code by adding inline, internal and external definitions of CSS and JavaScript code. Why we have so many different ways of adding foreign code into our HTML document will become more clear as we move forward.

Below we'll take a look at a piece of HTML code that demonstrates the following:

Line 4: Include external javascript file script.js
Line 5: Include external javascript file utility.js
Lines 6-9: Provide free space for writing internal JavaScript directly in your HTML document. This code typically executes at the same time while the webpage is actually downloading into the browser.
Lines 10-12: Include external CSS file style.css
Lines 13-15: Include internal CSS. Write directly into the HTML file.
Lines 18-21: Include internal CSS. Same as above but only inside <body> tag.
Lines 27-31: Include internal JavaScript at the very bottom of the page (different.)

```
1   <DOCTYPE html>
2   <html>
3     <head>
4       <script src = 'script.js' type = "text/javascript"></
              script>
5       <script src = 'utility.js' type = "text/javascript"></
              script>
6       <script type = "text/javascript">
7         var text = "Hello_there.";
8         var number = 1;
9       </script>tb
10      <link rel = "stylesheet"
11            type = "text/css"
12            href = "style.css">
13      <style type = "text/css">
14        #list { color: blue; }
15      </style>
16    <head>
17    <body>
18      <style type = "text/css" scoped>
19        body { background: white; }
20        #list { color: red; }
21      </style>
22      <ul id = "list">
```

```
23          <li>First item on my list</li>
24          <li>Second item on my list</li>
25          <li>Third item on my list</li>
26       </ul>
27        <script type = "text/javascript">
28           var text = "Hello there again. Secret number is =";
29           var number = 10;
30           console.log(text + number);
31        </script>
32     </body>
33  </html>
```

This is a slightly more advanced example of mixing HTML, CSS and JavaScript. The purpose of this example is to demonstrate the places within an HTML document where it's possible to write code written in languages other than HTML, because they are so commonly used together.

Note that according to HTML4, an older version of HTML <style> is not allowed within <body> tag. Even though placing it there would not generate an error or break your page design in any way. It would still work because most browsers support it against the specification rules. This is why it's still a good habit to try and keep CSS and JavaScript within <head> tab whenever possible.

In HTML5, however, a tag property called scoped was added. Adding it to style tag itself makes specifying <style> tags within <body> legal. This doesn't really change a lot because as we mentioned earlier writing CSS code without scoped property will still work in both HTML4 and HTML5.

While these types of details are important if you're interested in writing valid HTML code, HTML itself is a very forgiving language. Some mistakes will not affect the way your design is actually displayed in the browser. This can be a good and a bad thing. It's just something to be mindful of.

And finally, notice on lines 027-031 here JavaScript is included internally but just before the closing </body> tag. Remember that internal JavaScript is executed simultaneously as the webpage continues to download into the browser. Including JavaScript at the very bottom ensures that most HTML elements will be loaded into the browser before any JavaScript is executed. This prevents a situation where your JavaScript is trying to access an HTML element that has not yet loaded into the browser. In almost every case this will generate a JavaScript error which will result in all consequent JavaScript execution come to a halt, regardless if there was more JavaScript statements to execute.

`<link>`, `<style>` and `<script>` tags can use HTML attributes just the same like any other element. In case where they refer to another language they need to specify the format of that language to tell the browser about which type of content will be used within that tag.

Let's take a closer look:

1. Specify external CSS file: "style.css":

```
<link type = "text/css" href = "style.css">
```

2. Attribute value "text/javascript" means that content of this tag is JavaScript code:

```
<script type = "text/javascript"></script>
```

3. The "text/css" value informs us that this tag contains internal CSS code embedded directly into HTML document:

```
<style type = "text/css"></style>
```

4. Same as above but scoped to the enclosing parent tag:

```
<style type = "text/css" scoped></style>
```

Other than "text/css" and "text/javascript" HTML provides a few other possible content types. But at this point, we are not concerned with them. For example advanced types such as "WebGL shaders" are useful for making 3D games on HTML canvas tag. But this is not covered by the scope of this book.

2 Chapter II - Working With Color

One of the first questions a web designer learning HTML for the first time will inevitably ask is: *"How can I change color of a particular HTML element?"*

2.1 The Basics

When HTML language came out for the first time in the 90's, color was usually set directly through HTML attributes `color` and `background`:

```
<body background = "black" color = "white">Hello there, this
    is my webpage</body>
```

Or an equivalent, using the same colors but in *hexadecimal* format:

```
<body background = "#000000" color = "#ffffff">Hello there,
    this is my webpage</body>
```

Notice that we are assigning attributes to the `<body>` tag, which is the parent container element of the entire page. Therefore, these examples demonstrate how to invert the default background color of a web page (white) to black and change text color to white.

This looks simple enough. But don't rush to use these in your own code just yet!

These *deprecated* features were later completely replaced by CSS (*Cascading Style Sheets*) implementation. In modern HTML the attributes `background`, `color` and others have been moved to CSS (*Cascading Style Sheets*).

We've learned from a previous chapter that CSS can be applied to HTML elements by specifying it as a value of the `style` attribute. For instance, to produce the same inverted colors from examples above they can (and *should*) be assigned to an HTML element using the following CSS:

```
<body style = "background:_black;_color:_white">
    Hello there.</body>
```

Or using *hexadecimal* (more on this shortly) values:

```
<body style = "background:_#000;_color:_#fff">
    Hello there.</body>
```

2.2 HTML Elements And Cascading Style Sheets

Although CSS is not primary subject of this book, it would be difficult to provide concrete examples of styling HTML elements without it. For example, text of a warning or alert message is commonly set to red or orange color. As we have just pointed out, in HTML color is usually specified in CSS language using the `style` attribute.

In this chapter, we have already taken a quick look at setting background and text colors to an HTMl element. We'll finish our discussion with a brief explanation of the Hexadecimal color format and setting the *border* color (and size) of HTML elements. By doing so we will briefly touch on CSS, an integral part of styling HTML.

Note that you should always think of HTML and CSS separately. HTML should be used to provide only the hierarchical structure of elements in your document. CSS is layered on top of that structure to modify visual appearance of those elements.

Another reason for including CSS in an HTML book is because literally none of the websites you will browse today are ever constructed merely of HTML alone. If we never talked about CSS, it would be difficult to make examples in this book look interesting enough or resemble their application in a real-world scenario.

2.3 Understanding Hexadecimal Values

Let's start with doing a brief review of how color works in HTML. In HTML common colors already have named values such as "red", "black", "brown", "purple" and so on... ready to be used.

But these colors limit us only to the named colors provided by HTML. To get a full range of colors we must use a slightly advanced color system represented by numbers stored in hexadecimal format.

Just like in the familiar decimal system where numbers range between 0-10, in hexadecimal format, we use values between 0-15 to represent a number. Except instead of using digits 10-15 we use letters A, B, C, D, E and F respectively.

Figure 15: Just like in the decimal numbering system that ranges between 0-9, numbers in Hexadecimal format range from 0 to F. The letters A, B, C, D, E and F represent digits 10 - 15 in decimal system.

And here are some random examples of colors specified using hexadecimal format. Note that the # character is decorative. But it's necessary to use it when passing colors in hexadecimal format as values to CSS properties.

Black	#000000
Blue	#FF0000
Green	#33FF00
Brown	#663300
Violet	#9933FF
Purple	#CC33FF
Teal	#99FFFF
Cherry	#CC0000
Red	#FF0000
Orange	#FF3300
Yellow	#FFFF00

Figure 16: A few colors represented by their equivalent value in hexadecimal format.

A pair of two hexadecimal digits (0 to F) can be used to represent exactly 256 values between 0 - 255 (note, counting starts with 0, not 1). But how does HTML really know how to generate a color from values in this format?

Two hexadecimal digits can be used to represent one single color channel (Red, Green or Blue). Therefore, the value consisting of 6 hexadecimal digits contains enough data to represent a single color by forming a RGB composite value!

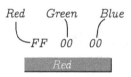

Figure 17: Red in hexadecimal format consists of 255 (#FF) for red channel and 0 (#00) for both green and blue channels.

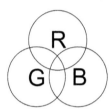

Figure 18: Hexadecimal format helps us break colors down in 3 unique channels: Red, Green and Blue. This gives you complete control over the full range of colors it's possible to create using this format.

Red Green Blue		Hexadecimal			Named	Decimal 0−255
00 00 00	=	000000	=	000	= BLACK	RGB(0, 0, 0)
FF FF FF	=	FFFFFF	=	FFF	= WHITE	RGB(255,255,255)
FF 00 00	=	FF0000	=	F00	= RED	RGB(255, 0, 0)
00 FF 00	=	00FF00	=	0F0	= GREEN	RGB(0,255, 0)
00 00 FF	=	0000FF	=	00F	= BLUE	RGB(0, 0,255)
80 80 00	=	808000	=	880	= OLIVE	RGB(128,128, 0)
00 80 80	=	008080	=	088	= TEAL	RGB(0,128,128)

Figure 19: In HTML, you can pass color values represented in any of the 4 different ways shown on this diagram to the **style** attribute of an element in parameters that accept color as a value.

The four color formats are 1. Hexadecimal, 2. Hexadecimal shortened to three digits, 3. Named colors (red, blue, black, etc.) and 4. by using the RGB macro that takes Red, Green and Blue channel values as numbers in decimal format between 0 - 255. It's up to you how you wish to specify colors for your elements.

Using one format consistently throughout your HTML documents is ideal for keeping your code uniform and easy to read.

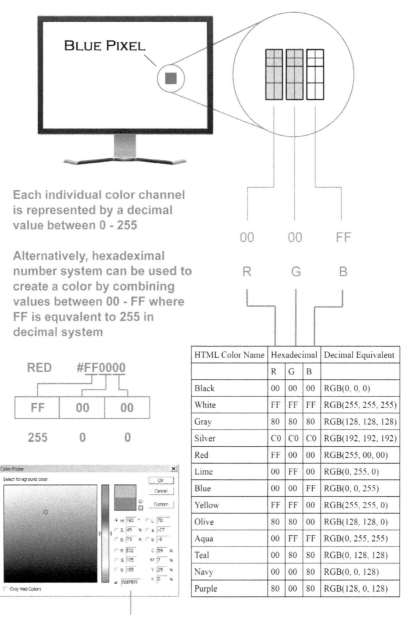

Figure 20: Switching the color of a pixel on your monitor to blue consists of juggling around the R (red), G (green), B (blue) values. In this case, we want to turn R and G values to 0 and switch the blue channel (B) all the way up to its highest possible value of (255) or #FF in hexadecimal format.

Hexadecimal values provide 16,777,216 unique color values you can use to color elements on your website. It's rare for web designers to create HEX colors manually. Instead Photoshop or online color picker tools can be used to intuitively determine the value you're looking for.

2.4 Setting Background and Font Colors

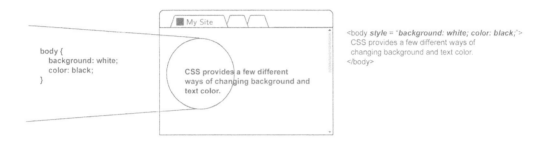

Figure 21: Using style attribute of an HTML element it is possible to modify its background and text colors.

The example above will produce the default web page look: black text on white background, so you may not visually see any changes. But this is just an example!

Alternatively to using the style attribute, you can use the following CSS code:

```
body { background: white; color: black; }
```

In that case, the code above should be placed between `<style></style>` tags nested within `<head>` tags in your HTML document as mentioned in a previous chapter.

Of course setting background and text color is not limited just to the body HTML tag. It will work in exactly the same way on any other HTML element.

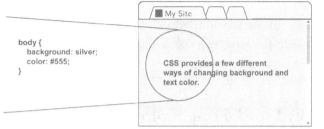

```
body {
    background: silver;
    color: #555;
}
```

```
<body style = "background: silver; color: #555;">
CSS provides a few different ways of
changing background and text color.
</body>
```

CSS provides a few different ways of changing background and text color.

Figure 22: Likewise, we can set our web page background color to "silver", a named HTML color. In Hexadecimal "silver" color is represented by #C0C0C0. Using the RGB macro, you can also specify it as RGB(192, 192, 192). This basically means that setting the average of 192 to each color channel (red, green and blue), a light grayish color will be produced since the value of light is distributed equally.

```
body { background: silver; }
body { background: #C0C0C0; }
body { color: #333; }
```

The text color in this example is set to #333. It is a dark gray color that is the equivalent of #303030 in Hexadecimal format. HTML accepts shorter representation of the same color. In the case of gray and few other colors (for example red can be represented as #FF0000 as well as #F00) it makes sense shortening the value to 3 digits without losing color precision. Here the color will be "scaled" to less color possibilities without losing precision. But in other cases, it may not be possible, because #000000 format gives you the highest precision over color contrast in each channel. For example, it is impossible to represent the color #CF0000 using only 3 digits (The closest you could end up with either #C00 or #F00 which are visibly different colors.)

Figure 23: You can also set background and text colors to any element within your HTML document. In this example, an arbitrary DIV element is present, positioned somewhere in the middle of the screen.

Positioning individual HTML elements on your page will be covered throughout the rest of this book.

```
<body style = "background: #000000; color: #808000">
<body style = "background: #000; color: #880">
<body style = "background: black; color: olive">
```

Figure 24: Setting background and color of the BODY element by inserting "inline" CSS directly into style attribute.

```
color: RGB(0, 0, 0)
color: #000000
color: #000
color: black
```

Figure 25: Setting font color to black in four different ways. They all create the same color: "black" represented by four different color formats.

background-color: RGB(255,255,255)	*same as*	background: RGB(255,255,255)
background-color: #FFFFFF	*same as*	background: #FFFFFF
background-color: #FFF	*same as*	background-color: #FFF
background-color: white	*same as*	background-color: white

Figure 26: You can also use background-color instead of background property. The background property is often used to provide a full scope of properties to how you wish to handle element's background, including using an image instead of a color value.

2.5   Using Single CSS Property To Set Multiple Values

Some HTML elements contain multiple values for the same property. This is why CSS properties can be set individually. For example background-color is only the color component of the background property. To demonstrate, let's break down the background property into individal composite values:

```
background-color: #000000;
background-image: url(image.png);
background-position: top left;
background-repeat: no-repeat;
background-size: 100% 100%;
```

There are a few others, but we're not concerned with them at this moment.

We can rewrite the code above into the full composite of the CSS background property. The following format is also completely acceptable by CSS processing engine:

```
background: #000000 url(image.png) top left no-repeat;
```

Here we set background *color*, background image *URL source*, *position* background image to start in upper left corner, and finally tell the element not to "repeat" the background image if the size of the element is larger than the original size of the image. All of this is done by assigning multiple values to just a single CSS property called: **background**.

Many other CSS properties can be set in this way, as well as individually. The background-repeat property can also be set to "no-repeat" for example, if you wanted to single it out. In addition other CSS properties such as borders, padding and margins of an element follow a similar pattern. We'll take a look at how this works in practice and in much greater detail in the following sections of this book.

We're not concerned with images until one of the next chapters. But it's nice to know at this point that it's also possible to assign a JPG or PNG image as a background of an HTML element (instead of, or in addition to a solid color) via the `background` CSS property.

2.6   Setting Element's Border Color

Following a similar principle of CSS property composition let's take a look at how we can also set color to an element's border.

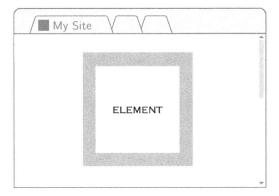

Figure 27: Imagine that we have an arbitrary HTML element positioned somewhere in the middle of our page. This can be a DIV, a TABLE or any other HTML element.

```
border-width: 10px;
border-color: gray;
border-style: solid;
```

Figure 28: To specify the color of the border, we must first construct it using these three CSS properties: border-width, border-style and finally set the color with border-color.

```
border: 10px solid gray;
```

Figure 29: To save space, CSS provides this shorthand version where you can specify width, color and style of the border all in one property value: 10px solid gray. Here "solid" stands for the type of the border you wish to draw around the element. For example setting this property to "dashed" would produced a dashed-line border. Or "dotted" for a dotted line.

Because "dashed" and "dotted" lines are implemented differently in browsers they are sort of a bad practice when it comes to web design. If you wish to create a dotted or a dashed border around your element (which in itself is a rare case) and want to ensure that it looks the same in all browsers, you might need to use custom images or construct it from multiple DIV elements.

3   Chapter III – Color Gradients

Gradients can be used for a variety of reasons. But the most common thing they're usually used for is to provide a smooth shading effect across the area of some User Interface element.

Here are a couple more reasons for using them:

Smooth Background Color Shading provides an elegant solution for making your HTML elements more appealing to the eye.

Saving Bandwidth is another benefit of using gradients, because they are automatically generated in browser by an efficient color shading algorithm. This means that they can be used instead of images, which would otherwise take a lot longer to download from the web server.

Simple Definitions can be used in `background` property to create some quite interesting and sometimes surprising effects. You will be supplying the minimum required parameters to either `linear-gradient` or `radial-gradient` properties to create any of the effects demonstrated in the next section.

3.1   Birds-Eye View

In this chapter we will learn how to create these gradients in HTML:

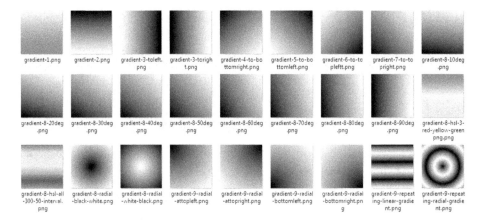

Figure 30: If this is a black and white print, you will not see the difference between gradients that actually use color. However, to master gradients you really only need a good grasp on their direction and type of which there are four – `linear-gradient`, `radial-gradient`, `repeating-linear-gradient` and `repeating-radial-gradient`. This diagram gives you a good idea of the variety of gradients it is possible to create for your HTML elements with CSS.

I cheated a little here... the images above are files from my gradients folder that I created while working on this book. But how do we actually create them using CSS commands? The rest of this chapter will provide a solution!

3.2 Choosing an Arbitrary HTML Element for Displaying Gradients

We will perform our experiments with the background gradients using this simple DIV element. Let's set some basic properties to it first, including width=500px and height=500px.

For now, we just need a simple square element. Paste this code anywhere in between `<head>` tags in your HTML document.

```
<style type = "text/css">
  div {
```

46

```
    position: relative;
    display: block;
    width: 500px;
    height: 500px;
  }
<style>
```

This CSS code will turn every `<div>` element on the screen to a square with dimensions of 500 by 500 pixels. The `position` and `display` properties will be explained further in the book.

Alternatively, we probably want to assign gradients only to one HTML element. In which case you can either specify the CSS to an individual `div` element using a unique ID such as `#my-gradient-box` *or any other that makes sense to you.*

```
<style type = "text/css">
div#my-gradient-box { position: relative; display: block;
    width: 500px; height: 500px; }
<style>
```

And then add it somewhere within your `<body>` tag as:

```
<!-- Experimenting with Color Gradient Backgrounds in HTML
    //-->
<div id = "my-gradient-box"></div>
```

Or type the same CSS commands directly into `style` attribute of an HTML element you wish to apply a color gradient to:

```
<div style = "position:_relative;_display:_block;_width:_500
    px;_height:_500px;"></div>
```

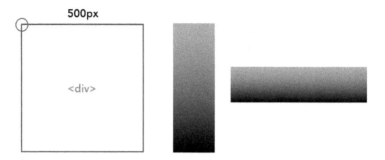

Figure 31: A div element with dimension of 500 x 500 pixels. The row and column on the right hand side demonstrate how gradients automatically adapt to the element's size. The gradient property was not changed here. Only the elements dimensions, yet the gradient looks quite different. Keep this in mind when making your own gradients!

CSS gradients will automatically adapt to the elements width and height. *Which might produce a slightly different effect.*

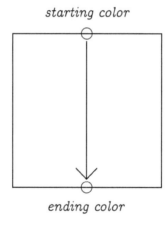

Figure 32: The basic idea behind gradients is to interpolate between at least two colors. By default, without providing any extra values, vertical direction is assumed. The starting color will begin at the top of the element, gradually blending in with 100% of the second color at the bottom. It's possible to create gradients by combining more than two colors. We'll take a look at that in a moment!

All CSS gradient values are supplied to CSS `background` property!

Having said that, here's an example of creating a simple linear gradient:

```
backgroud: linear-gradient(black, white);
```

These values will be demonstrated in action below, shown just underneath the gradient effect they produce.

3.3   Gradient Types

Let's walk through different gradient styles one by one and visualize the type of gradient effects you would expect to be rendered within the HTML element, when these styles are applied to it.

linear-gradient(black, white)   *linear-gradient(yellow, red)*

Figure 33: A simple linear gradient. Left: black to white. Right: yellow to red.

linear-gradient(to left, black, white)   *linear-gradient(to right, black, white)*

Figure 34: Horizontal gradients can be created by specifying a leading value of either "to left" or "to right", depending on which direction you wish your gradient to flow across the element.

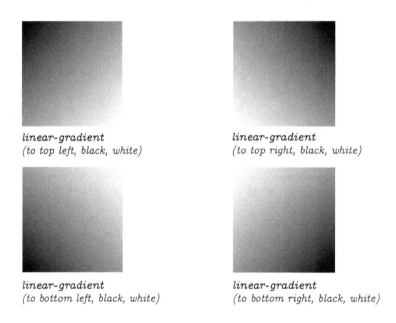

linear-gradient
(to top left, black, white)

linear-gradient
(to top right, black, white)

linear-gradient
(to bottom left, black, white)

linear-gradient
(to bottom right, black, white)

Figure 35: You can start gradients at corners too to create diagonal color transitions. Values "to top left", "to top right", "to bottom left" and "to bottom right" can be used to achieve that effect.

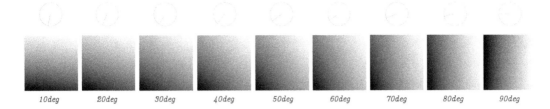

| 10deg | 20deg | 30deg | 40deg | 50deg | 60deg | 70deg | 80deg | 90deg |

Figure 36: When 45 degree corners are not enough, you can supply a custom degree between 0 – 360 directly to the `linear-gradient` property as in `linear-gradient(30deg, black, white);` Notice how in this example the gradient gradually changes direction from flowing toward the bottom, toward the left hand side when angle is changed in progression from 10 to 90 degrees.

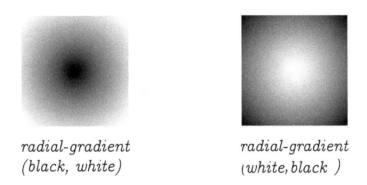

radial-gradient
(black, white)

radial-gradient
(white, black)

Figure 37: Radial gradients can be created by using `radial-gradient` property. Swapping colors around will produce an inverse effect.

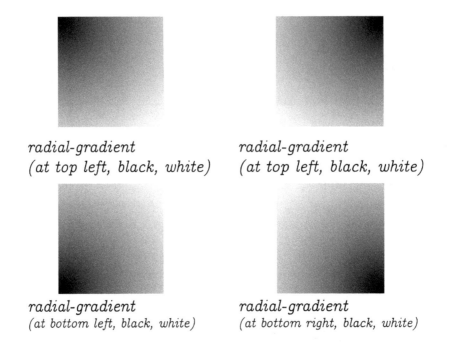

radial-gradient
(at top left, black, white)

radial-gradient
(at top left, black, white)

radial-gradient
(at bottom left, black, white)

radial-gradient
(at bottom right, black, white)

Figure 38: In the same way as linear gradients, radial gradients can also take origin at any of the four corners of an HTML element.

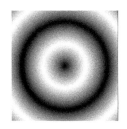

repeating-linear-gradient
(white 100px,
black 200px,
white 300px);

repeating-radial-gradient
(white 100px,
black 200px,
white 300px);

Figure 39: Repetitive patterns for linear and radial gradients can be created using `repeating-linear-gradient` and `repeating-radial-gradient` respectively. You can provide as many repetitive color values in a row as needed. Just don't forget to separate them by a comma!

linear-gradient
hsl(0,100%,50%),
hsl(50,100%,50%),
hsl(100,100%,50%),
hsl(150,100%,50%),
hsl(200,100%,50%),
hsl(250,100%,50%),
hsl(300,100%,50%)

linear-gradient
hsl(0,100%,50%),
hsl(50,100%,50%),
hsl(300,100%,50%)

Figure 40: Finally – the most advanced type of a gradient can be created using a series of HSL values. HSL values don't have named or RGB equivalents, they are counted on a scale from 0 – 300. See the explanation below.

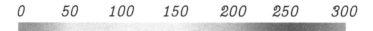

Figure 41: You can cherry-pick any color by using values between 0 – 300.

We've already provided examples of property values associated with each gradient. But here they are again in one place. Play around with the values and see what type of effects they produce on your custom UI elements:

```
background: linear-gradient(yellow, red);
background: linear-gradient(black, white);
background: linear-gradient(to right, black, white);
background: linear-gradient(to left, black, white);
background: linear-gradient(to bottom right, black, white);
background: linear-gradient(90deg, black, white);
background: linear-gradient(
    hsl(0,100%,50%),
    hsl(50,100%,50%),
    hsl(100,100%,50%),
    hsl(150,100%,50%),
    hsl(200,100%,50%),
    hsl(250,100%,50%),
    hsl(300,100%,50%));
background: radial-gradient(black, white);
background: radial-gradient(at bottom right, black, white);
background:
  repeating-linear-gradient
  (white 100px, black 200px, white 300px);
background:
  repeating-radial-gradient
  (white 100px, black 200px, white 300px);
```

4 Chapter IV – Text

Text is the most simple type of content in HTML.

In this section we will explore how to change appearance of HTML text by adjusting following properties: *Font Family, color,* and *size.*

4.1 Font Family

Font-family is just another way of referring to font style or font type, for example: *Arial, Verdana, Tahoma* or the default *Times New Roman.*

To set *Arial* as the font for text written inside the web page parent element `<body>` *and all of its children elements* you can use this CSS code:

```
body { font-family: Arial; }
```

To set *Verdana* as the font for absolutely all HTML elements in your document, you can use the star ("*") character:

```
* { font-family: Verdana; }
```

Although not absolutely necessary, HTML text is often enveloped in `<span>` tags. When this is the case, these span elements will inherit the width of the text contained within them and be treated as "inline" elements by default (*we'll explore inline elements in a lot more detail later in the book.*) The width of the span elements containing text is automatically determined by taking in consideration font's family and size.

Examples below demonstrate not only that, but also the fact that the upper left corner of span elements is counted as their origin point. For example, if you rotate this element around (*we'll take a look at this also later in the book,*) the element will be rotated around its upper left corner. Most other elements in HTML also share the upper left corner as the element's pivot. So from now on in the book if you see a small circle with a dot and arrows, it will indicate the assumed starting location point of the element. Why this is important will become more clear when we reach chapters on element positioning on the screen.

Let's take a look at some commonly used HTML fonts:

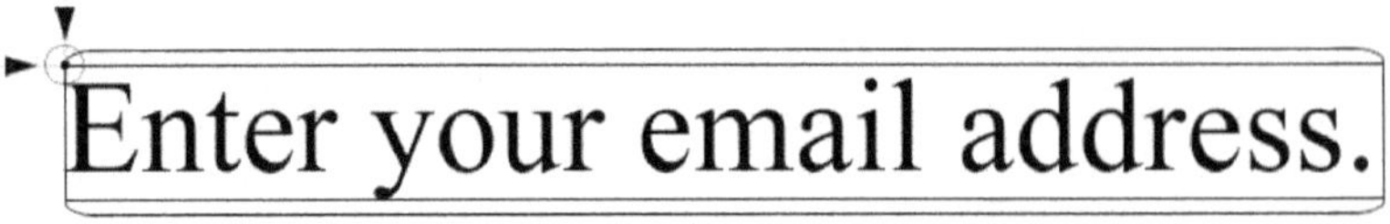

Figure 42: Times New Roman is the default font type in HTML.

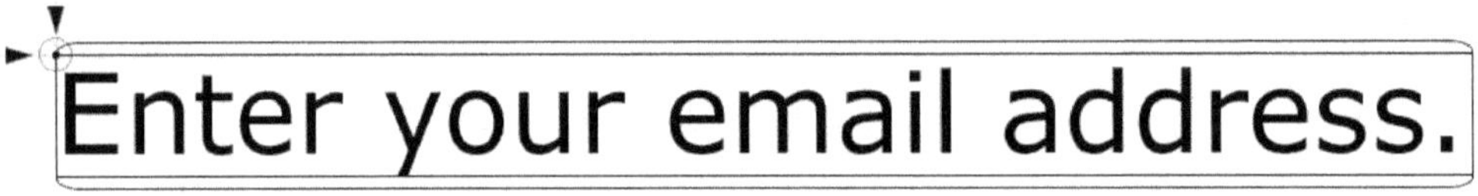

Figure 43: Verdana.

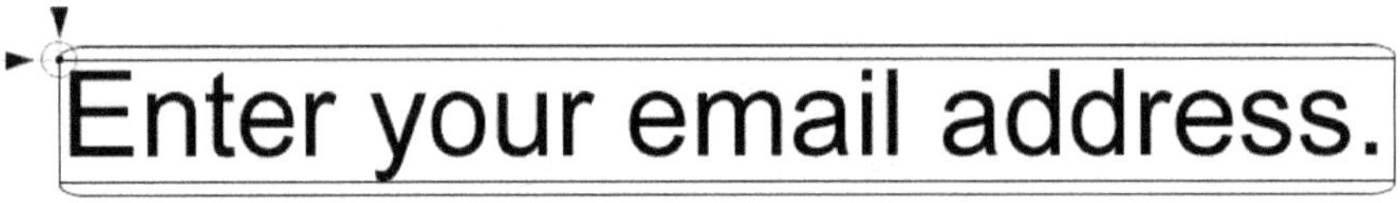

Figure 44: Arial. Google's favorite.

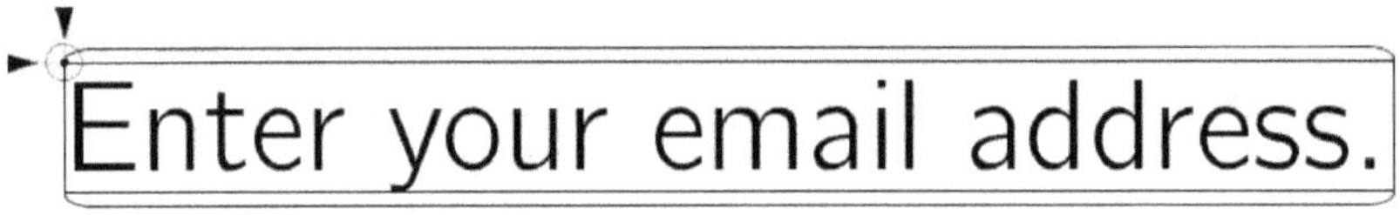

Figure 45: Computer Modern (The font this book was written in.)

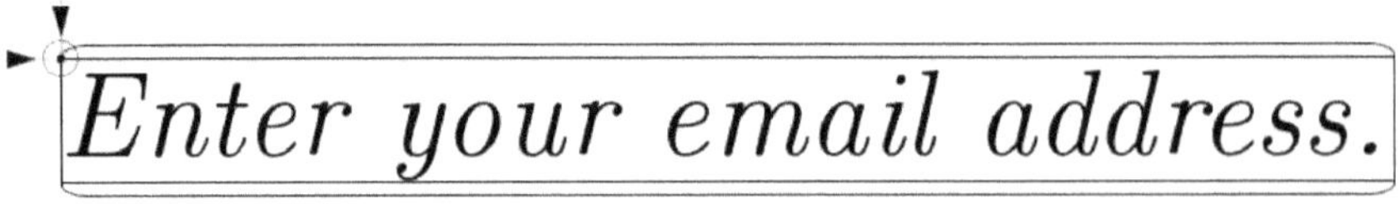

Figure 46: Computer Modern Classical.

Italic   Bold   Italic Bold   Regular

Figure 47: Sectioning text using span elements.

You can section text into blocks using different styles. Sometimes italicizing or making text bold becomes necessary.

4.2 Google Fonts

Arial, *Verdana* and *Courier* (for code listings) are all great fonts. But sometimes, the standard set provided by your Operating System is not sufficient for creating a particular impression. This is especially true when planning unique wire-frames for website layouts or user interfaces, where the style of text is part of the subtle impression created by the design itself.

Many beautiful fonts are available at `fonts.google.com` – the font repository created by Google.

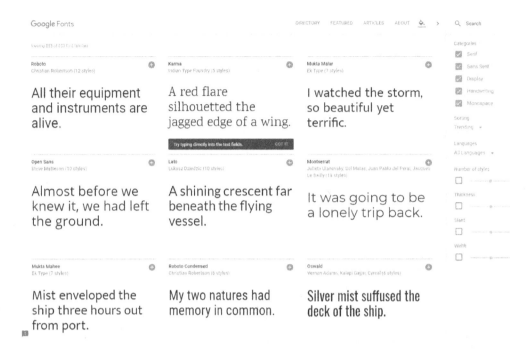

Figure 48: Point your browser at fonts.google.com to browse a set of alternative fonts from Google Fonts.

Select one or more fonts by clicking on the red plus button next to each. You will notice a new tab appearing toward the bottom of the screen. Click on the tab to open instructions on how to install selected fonts on your website:

Figure 49: The "Roboto" font was selected. The tab provides installation instructions.

Google Fonts come in different flavors. You can type your own phrases to see what they look like in the selected font before installing it. For example, here is what the title of this book looks like in several different manifestations of the "Roboto" font:

HTML: The Intuitive Guide
HTML: The Intuitive Guide
HTML: The Intuitive Guide
HTML: The Intuitive Guide
HTML: The Intuitive Guide
HTML: The Intuitive Guide
HTML: The Intuitive Guide
HTML: The Intuitive Guide
HTML: The Intuitive Guide
HTML: The Intuitive Guide
HTML: The Intuitive Guide
HTML: The Intuitive Guide

Figure 50: The title of this book rendered using the custom "Roboto" Google font.

Thin fonts are really great for achieving that "modern" look you see on many brand websites.

Embedding the font into your HTML code is a straightforward process. Copy and paste the `<link>` tag generated from this tab into your HTML document anywhere between `<head>` tags.

```
<link href="https://fonts.googleapis.com/css?family=
    Roboto" rel="stylesheet">
```

Every time you want to use "Roboto" font in your HTML, simply specify it as a value to the CSS property `font-family`.

4.3 Color

Changing font color is probably the easiest thing you can do in CSS. But Hexadecimal color values can be a little tricky to figure out, especially if you've never used them before.

```
<!-- Let's paint this paragraph's text blue //-->
<p style = "color:_blue;">A piece of text in blue.</p>

<!-- Same as above, except using a hexadecimal
    color value for "blue" //-->
<p style = "color:_#0000ff;">A piece of text in blue.</p>

<!-- Same as above, uppercase characters
    are allowed in hex format //-->
<p style = "color:_#0000FF;">A piece of text in blue.</p>

<!-- Same as above, but reduced to 3 digits
    (note; not all colors can be abbriviated this way) //--
    >
<p style = "color:_#00F;">A piece of text in blue.</p>
```

Luckily, we've already covered hexadecimal values in an earlier chapter *Chapter II – Working With Color.*

Head over there if you need a refresher!

4.4   Size

To set font size to a paragraph the `font-size` property is used:

```
<p style = "font-size:_12px;">
    This line of text will be displayed using a font
    with its size set to 12 pixels.</p>
```

In HTML it is possible to specify font size using **em** (*relative to capital M in typography*), **px** (*pixels*), **pt** (*points*) and **in** (*inches*).

It would be difficult to see the subtle difference these measurement units produce in comparison to each other without rendering some code in the browser. However, this diagram will hopefully make it a bit more clear:

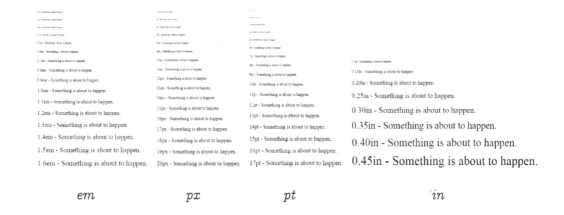

em   px   pt   in

Figure 51: Comparison between default HTML font *Times New Roman* and the way different measurement units affect its size.

They're all slightly different – but in general ***1em = 12pt = 16px = 100%***

The ***em*** in typography stood for the width of the capital letter M.

```
<p style = "font-size:⎵1.6em;">A line of text with
    font set in "em" typography unit.</p>
```

The most common unit, pixels or ***px*** is used to measure font size in pixels.

```
<p style = "font-size:⎵12px;">A line of text whose
    size is set in pixel units.</p>
```

A point or ***pt*** is a unit of measurement used for real life ink on paper typography.

```
<p style = "font-size:⎵17pt;">A line of text with its
    size set using point units.</p>
```

The ***in*** unit can be used to match your font size to the actual size of an inches on the screen, or its fraction.

```
<p style = "font-size:⎵0.25in;">A line of text with
    font size set to quarter of an inch.</p>
```

62

5 Chapter V – Hyperlinks

In HTML hyperlinks are clickable links that appear inside text blocks. Clicking on them will redirect your browser to the URL specified in the HREF attribute. It is my guess that HREF stands for Hyperlink Reference. This value can also be a DIV element's ID, and if such is the case, clicking on the link will move your browser view to the element matching that ID.

5.1 Creating Hyperlinks Using The Anchor Tag

Hyperlinks are created using the `<A>` HTML tag (which stands for *anchor*).

Amazon.com

Figure 52: This is what a hyperlink appears as in your HTML document. You see them all the time! But they also have a special purpose of linking your sites to other sites, or other web pages on your own domain name.

But how exactly do we create one? Below is an example of HTML code required to create a fully fledged hyperlink that also includes title text.

Specifying text in the extra `title` attribute is usually done to add detail to the *description of the page the hyperlink is pointing to*. Search engines are very clever at using this subtle information to categorize websites. So it is advised to spend an extra moment to decide what the title text should say. Use keywords or full sentences that describe the page the hyperlink is pointing to to the best of your ability. But don't forget to be as accurate as possible. Some of your page ranking on search engines such as Google depends on this!

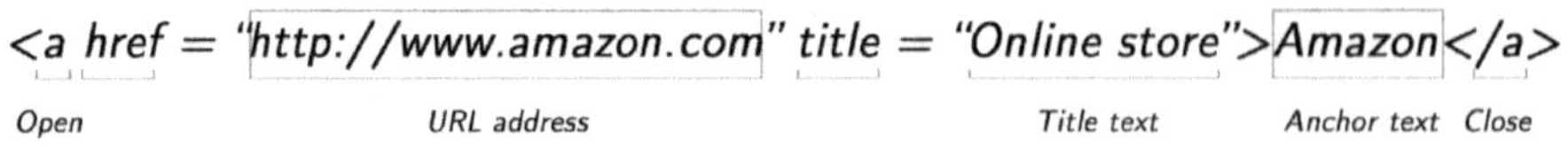

<a href = "http://www.amazon.com" title = "Online store">Amazon</a>

Open   URL address   Title text   Anchor text   Close

Figure 53: The composition of an HTML hyperlink. That's really all there is to it. Hyperlinks behave just like any other text elements. The only difference is that they are clickable and automatically inherit the "pointing hand" cursor.

5.2 Removing The Underline

Sometimes web designers remove the default text underline style from a hyperlink. You can easily achieve that by setting `text-decoration` property to "none":

```
<a href = "http://www.google.com"
   title = "Google search engine!"
   style = "text-decoration: none;">Google</a>
```

This will effectively remove the line underneath the hyperlink.

6 Chapter VI - Working With Images

In this chapter we will take a look at using images in your HTML document. There are two notably unique ways of using images in HTML.

First, you can use images as a background fill for an element. But you can also use images as individual blocking HTML elements, in the same way you would use a `<div>` or any other blocking element.

Background images fill the entire content area of an HTML element with a source image, instead of a solid color.

6.1 Background Images

Note: If the element's dimensions are bigger than those of the source image, the image will be repeated within the body of that element – repetitively filling the remainder of the element's sides with the contents of the image. It's almost like stretching infinite wall paper over an element. See example below:

Figure 54: The default background image behavior.

To set the background image to any element you can use the following CSS commands.

```
<!-- set background image to body //-->
<body style = "background: url('kitten.jpg')"></body>

<!-- or alternatively... //-->
<body style = "background-image: url('kitten.jpg')"></body>
```

You can also use internal CSS, placing this code between `<style></style>` tags:

```
body { background-image: url('kitten.jpg'); }
```

Or...

```
body { background: url('kitten.jpg'); }
```

6.1.1 no-repeat

Let's take a look at the same kitten background, except this time with `no-repeat` value set to `background-repeat` property;

You can prevent a background image from following its default behavior, by setting `background-repeat` property to the value of `no-repeat`, provided that the image was also already set via `background-image: url("kitten.jpg")`:

Figure 55: You can prevent the background image from repeating itself by setting either the individual property `background-repeat:  no-repeat` or together with the image source file `background:  url("kitten.jpg") no-repeat;`

6.1.2 background-size

The `background-size` property gives you control over the *size* of the background image. In particular, it is helpful when the image needs to be scaled across the element's dimensions. Different values will produce various tiling effects and patterns. They will be demonstrated in this section.

The background-size property takes following values: `unset`, `none`, `initial`, `auto`, `percent`, `percent percent` (*separated by space for* **x-axis** *and* **y-axis** *respectively,*) `cover` and `contain`:

background-size: unset;
background-size: none;
background-size: initial;
background-size: auto;

Figure 56: Default settings. Any of the values `unset`, `none`, `initial` and `auto` produce default behavior under standard circumstance.

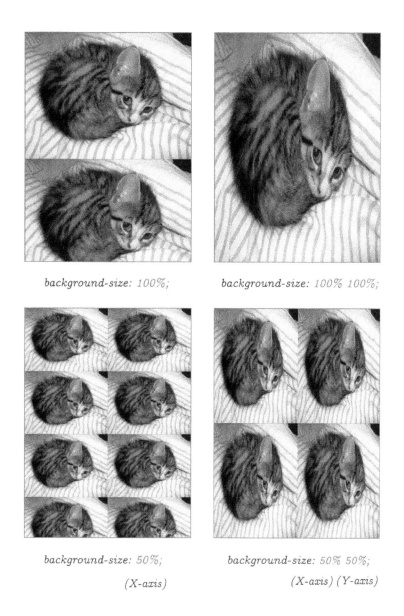

background-size: 100%;   *background-size: 100% 100%;*

background-size: 50%;   *background-size: 50% 50%;*

(X-axis)   *(X-axis) (Y-axis)*

Figure 57: `background-size` can optionally take *x-axis* and *y-axis* parameters separated by space character.

background-size: cover;　　　*background-size: contain;*

Figure 58: `cover` and `contain`.

Figure 59: By combining `background-repeat: no-repeat;` with `background-size: 100%` it is possible to stretch the image only horizontally, across the entire width of the element.

What if you want to repeat background vertically but keep it stretched across the width? No problem, simply remove `no-repeat` from previous example. This is what you will end up with:

Figure 60: This is really useful if you need to blow up a large image across the screen without sacrificing vertical repeat.

Sometimes it is needed to stretch the image across to fit the bounding box of an element. This often comes at a price of some distortion, however:

Figure 61: `background-size:   100% 100%`

Note here, 100% 100% is repeated twice. The first value tells CSS to "stretch the image vertically", the second 100% does the same horizontally. In HTML, whenever you need to specify multiple values, they are often separated by a space. Vertical coordinates always come first.

6.1.3   object-fit: fill—cover—contain—none

Cover and *contain* values from previous section can also be used on HTML elements such as images, videos and similar media. In this case, when `cover` and `contain` are used with `object-fit` CSS property, behavior of these elements follows rules demonstrated in the diagrams below:

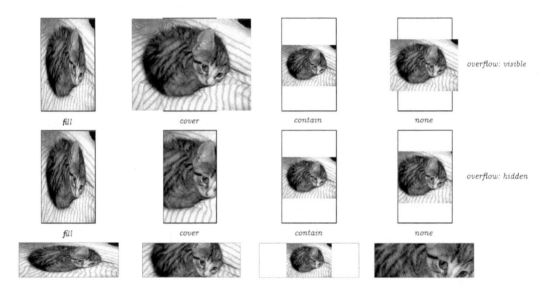

Figure 62: `fill`, `cover`, `contain` and `none` produce similar results to background-size property, except they work on HTML media elements, rather than background images.

6.1.4 background-position

Figure 63: Center on the screen without repeat can be achieved by combining `background-repeat:  no-repeat` and `background-position:  center center;`

In another scenario you can force the image to be always in the center and keep the repeat:

Figure   64:   `background-position: center center;`   with `background-repeat:  repeat;`

6.1.5 repeat-x

You can repeat the image across the x-axis only (horizontally) using **repeat-x**:

Figure 65: CSS style: `background-position: center center;` `background-repeat: repeat-x;`

6.1.6 repeat-y

To the same effect but on the y-axis **repeat-y** property can be used:

Figure 66: The `background-repeat` property set to **repeat-y**

Like any other CSS property, you have to juggle around the values to achieve the results you want. I think we covered pretty much everything there is about backgrounds. Except one last thing...

6.1.7 Multiple Backgrounds

It is possible to add more than one background to the same HTML element. The process is rather simple.

Consider these images stored in two separate files:

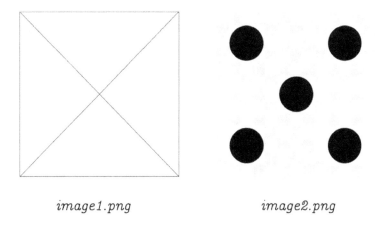

image1.png   *image2.png*

Figure 67: Two images that will be used for creating multiple backgrounds.

The chessboard pattern in the image on the right is only used to indicate *transparency* here. The white and grayish squares are not an actual part of the image itself. This is the "see-through" area, which you would usually see in digital manipulation software.

When the image on the right is placed on top of other HTML elements or images, the checkered area will not block that content underneath. And this is the whole idea behind multiple backgrounds in HTML.

6.1.8 Image Transparency

To fully take advantage of multiple backgrounds, one of the background images should have a transparent area. But how do we create one?

In this example, the second image (*image2.png*) contains 5 black dots on a transparent background (*indicated by a checkered pattern.*)

Figure 68: To create images with transparent backgrounds, tools such as Photoshop can be used. Just select the Magic Eraser tool from the toolbox.

Like many other CSS properties that accept multiple values – all you have to do – to set up multiple backgrounds is to provide a *set of values* to the `background` property separated by comma.

6.1.9 Specifying multiple background images

To assign multiple (layered) background images to the same HTML element, the following CSS can be used:

```
body { background: url('image2.png'), url('image1.png');
    }
```

The order in which you supply images to the background's url property is important. Note that the top-most image is always listed first. This is why we start with *image2.png*

This code produces the following result:

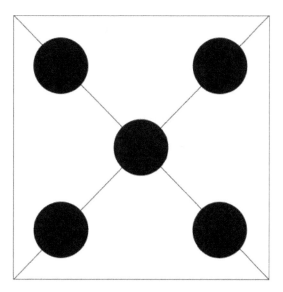

Figure 69: Multiple background in use. Here `image2.png` is superimposed on top of `image1.png`.

In this example we demonstrated multiple backgrounds in theory on a subjective `<div>` (or similar) element with square dimensions. Let's take a look at another example:

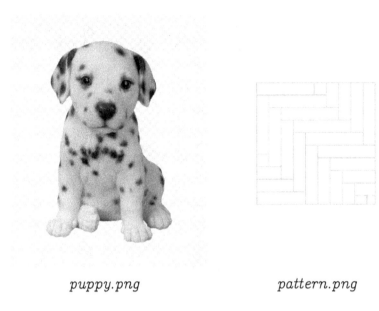

puppy.png   *pattern.png*

Figure 70: A puppy and a linoleum-like pattern.

Note here again, that the puppy.png image will be the first item on the comma-separated list. This is the image we want to *superimpose* on top of all of the other images on the list.

Combining the two:

```
body { background: url('puppy.png'), url('pattern.png');
    }
```

We get the following result:

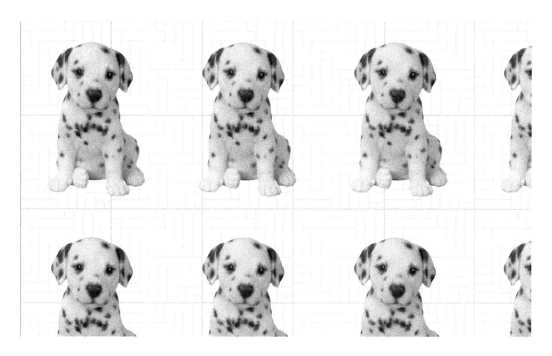

Figure 71: Multiple backgrounds.

6.1.10 Other background properties that take comma-separated lists

In the same way, you can supply other parameters to each individual background, using the other background properties demonstrated below:

```
background
background-attachment
background-clip
background-image
background-origin
background-position
background-repeat
background-size
```

The following property cannot be used with a list, for obvious reasons:

```
background-color
```

What would it mean to provide multiple color values to a background? Whenever color background property is set, it usually fills the entire area with a solid color. Therefore, it cannot be used in the case of multiple backgrounds for any meaningful purpose.

6.2 Images As HTML Elements

When I started working with HTML images, for some reason I always thought that they were completely separate entities from your standard HTML elements such as `<div>` for example. Perhaps this is because images by nature are so much more impressive than text content.

The *Morris Marina* is a car that was manufactured by Austin-Morris division of British Leyland from 1971 until 1980.

Figure 72: A simple image `<img = "auto.png" alt = "Morris Marina">` specimen that we will use to demonstrate working with images in HTML in this chapter.

I was wrong. The image element in HTML that can be used as `<image>` or `<img>` is just like any other HTML element. The only difference is the content area, which now contains an image, instead of text.

To prove that, here is an image with border, padding and margin set to some arbitrary values:

Figure 73: An image is just like any other blocking element containing *border*, *padding*, and *margin*. To be precise, an image is actually an inline *and* blocking element at the same time. In other words `display: inline-block`.

If you set any HTML element's `display` property to `inline-block` that element will behave exactly like an HTML image, even if it contains some other type of content inside.

One of the most common placement for images is in the middle of the page.

Figure 74: An image with `img {margin: auto}` margin set to *auto*.

Automatic margins will ensure that the image is aligned to the center of the page, and if there is any text surrounding the image it will appear above or below it, based on where it is located in your HTML document.

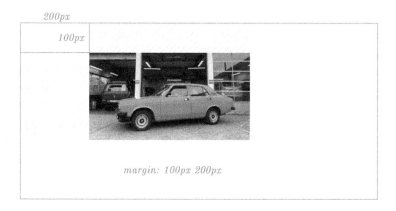

200px

100px

margin: 100px 200px

Figure 75: Margin property can be used to position an image within its parent.

The example above assumes that the image's `display` property is set to `block` and its position is set to `relative`.

Image margins are often used to bump text away from the image to create more white space, making the surrounding text easier to read.

But images can be also positioned using `display: block` and `position: absolute` combo. You just need to provide additional values for `top` and `left` properties to define its precise location on the screen *relative to its parent element.*

The above example can be interpreted as though the image's top/left properties were set to `top: 100px` and `left: 200px` to position it within parent element at exactly the same spot without having to do it via the margin property. Which is often the preferred way of doing it.

Note: In order for any HTML element to be accurately positioned within its parent container element using absolute pixel location the *parent element* is required to set its `display` property to a value of either `absolute` or `relative`. If you fail to do this, the behavior of the child element is unpredictable. But it will be most likely positioned relative to the root parent element such as `<body>`.

6.3   Changing Image Properties

For examples in this section, let's use another image of this barn owl.

Figure 76: `owl.png`

Figure 77: Owl image with padding, margin and border.

6.4   Stretching and Rotating Images

To stretch an image, simply specify its width property to a number in pixels or percent. If the value is larger than the original width of the image it will appear stretched:

Figure 78: width: 200%

Likewise, it is possible to stretch an image vertically using `height` property.

Figure 79: `height:   200%`

Around 2016 images with round corners started to be in wide use on social network websites:

Figure 80: `border:  4px solid black` and `border-radius:  16px`

As of the writing of this book – most social network profiles have turned to the round image appearance displayed below:

Figure 81: Turning a square image into a circle by maxing out `border-radius` property. here we also set `border:  4px solid black` for a slightly more dramatic effect.

This look can be achieved by maxing out the `border-radius` property. Setting it to an unrealistically high value such as `1000px` will ensure that images whose dimensions are less or equal to `1000px` will appear as circles.

You should probably set it to the actual width height of the image if you are absolutely sure that it will never be shown in larger size.

Figure 82: `transform:  rotate(45deg)`

Rotating an image is as simple as providing a degree of rotation in percent 0–360. The value must be post-fixed by "deg".

Figure 83: `float:  left`

In newspaper articles, it is common to move the image left or right, so it doesn't interfere with the text in the body of the article. To achieve this we can assign the `float` property to the image with a value of either `left` or `right`.

Figure 84: `float:  right`

But `float` property will not save us from creating enough space between text and the image. For this reason we can additionally use the image's `margin-left` or `margin-right` property.

Figure 85: Using additional margin (`margin-left:  16px`) we can add more spacing between the image and the surrounding text.

7 Chapter VII - Tables

7.1 If You Can't Use a Desk Use a Table

Tables are used to display tabular data. Similar to an Excel spreadsheet tables display information by treating it as rows and columns.

Tags `<tr>` and `<td>` are required to be nested within `<table>` tag, and cannot and should not be ever used outside of it. They are responsible for creating blocks of elements that help with construction of a table where `<tr>` represents a row and `<td>` represents a column.

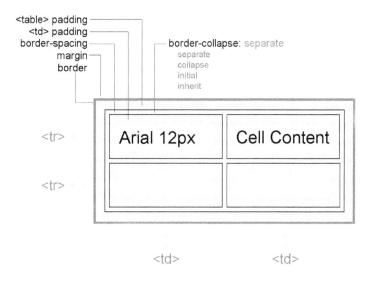

Figure 86: Basic structure of a table element.

Let's create a basic table displaying Top 10 Albums of All Time:

```
1  <h1>Top 10 Albums of All Time</h1>
2  <table>
3    <!-- First row, header information //-->
4    <tr>
5      <td>Position</td>
6      <td>Album</td>
```

```
7       <td>Artist</td>
8     </tr>
9     <!-- Consequent rows listing music albums //-->
10    <tr>
11      <td>1</td>
12      <td>Dark Side of the Moon</td>
13      <td>Pink Floyd</td>
14    </tr>
15    <tr>
16      <td>2</td>
17      <td>Sgt. Pepper's Lonely Hearts Club Band</td>
18      <td>The Beatles</td>
19    </tr>
20    <tr>
21      <td>3</td>
22      <td>Led Zeppelin IV (aka ZOSO)</td>
23      <td>Led Zeppelin</td>
24    </tr>
25    <tr>
26      <td>4</td>
27      <td>Abbey Road</td>
28      <td>The Beatles</td>
29    </tr>
30    <tr>
31      <td>5</td>
32      <td>The Wall</td>
33      <td>Pink Floyd</td>
34    </tr>
35    <tr>
36      <td>6</td>
37      <td>Nevermind</td>
38      <td>Nirvana</td>
39    </tr>
40    <tr>
41      <td>7</td>
42      <td>Revolver</td>
43      <td>The Beatles</td>
44    </tr>
```

```
45    <tr>
46      <td>8</td>
47      <td>A Night at the Opera</td>
48      <td>Queen</td>
49    </tr>
50    <tr>
51      <td>9</td>
52      <td>Ok Computer</td>
53      <td>Radiohead</td>
54    </tr>
55    <tr>
56      <td>10</td>
57      <td>Pet Sounds</td>
58      <td>The Beach Boys</td>
59    </tr>
60  </table>
```

This HTML table code will produce the following output:

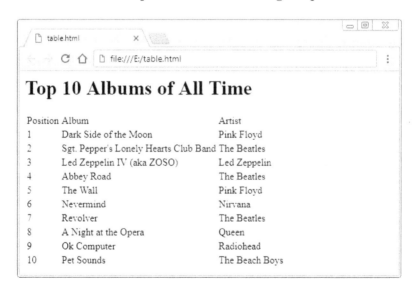

Figure 87:

Creating HTML tables using the structure defined by nested <tr> and <td> tags as was shown in this example is a straightforward process.

7.2 Using <thead>, <tbody> and <tfoot>

Additional table-related HTML elements exist <thead>, <tbody> and <tfoot>, all three of which are used in conjunction with each other. They determine purpose of a specific area in your table. These tags are optional and rarely used in construction of HTML tables. Nonetheless, they might be useful for improving structural integrity of your tables.

```
1  <table>
2
3    <thead>
4      <tr>
5        <td>November</td>
6        <td>2 ft.</td>
7      </tr>
8    </thead>
9
10   <tbody>
11     <tr>
12        <td>December</td>
13        <td>3 ft.</td>
14      </tr>
15   </tbody>
16
17   <tfoot>
18     <tr>
19        <td>Total</td>
20        <td>5 ft.</td>
21      </tr>
22   </tfoot>
23
24 </table>
```

Regardless where in nesting hierarchy <thead> or <tfoot> are specified, they will always appear in their proper place when rendered in the browser. The correct order is retained. For example, consider this intentionally jumbled up order:

```
1  <table>
```

```
2        <tfoot>foot</tfoot>   <!-- tfoot first //-->
3        <thead>head</thead>   <!-- thead second //-->
4        <tbody>body</tbody>   <!-- tbody third //-->
5   </table>
```

Nonetheless, when viewed in browser, the rows will still be rendered in the proper order:

− head
− body
− foot

We've just summarized the process of creating structure for simple tables. You may want to experiment by creating a few of your own. In the next section, we'll take a look at improving the visual appearance of our tables using Cascading Style Sheets.

7.3   Decorating HTML Tables

We've just considered a few basic HTML tables. But they look plain and a bit boring. When designing real websites you will probably want to decorate your table to make them look less visually desolate.

Let's write some very basic CSS to change the look of any HTML `<table>` and make it appear as though it has a lining of 1 pixel in width around its border and the cells within it.

```
1  <style type="text/css">
2       table { border-collapse: collapse; }
3       table, th, tr, td { border: 1px solid black; }
4       table td { font-family: Arial; font-size: 12px; padding:
             4px; }
5  </style>
```

Here CSS style `border-collapse: collapse;` will make sure that there are no "double" borders between each cell in the table. A better font (Arial is a good font, in my opinion) and some cell padding has been added to `<td>` tags.

It's interesting how just simple tweaks to the styling of HTML elements can produce significant updates to the overal look and feel:

Position	Album	Artist
1	Dark Side of the Moon	Pink Floyd
2	Sgt. Pepper's Lonely Hearts Club Band	The Beatles
3	Led Zeppelin IV (aka ZOSO)	Led Zeppelin
4	Abbey Road	The Beatles
5	The Wall	Pink Floyd
6	Nevermind	Nirvana
7	Revolver	The Beatles
8	A Night at the Opera	Queen
9	Ok Computer	Radiohead
10	Pet Sounds	The Beach Boys

Figure 88:

This looks a lot more readable, compared to the "default" style-less HTML table. All this was accomplishes by specifying just a few CSS commands within `<style>` tag.

7.4   Oh, And One More Thing About `<th>` Tag

Up to this point we used `<thead>` tag to specify table header placement. And it is the proper tag to use when it is used together with `<tbody>` and `<tfoot>`. In fact it is assumed that you use all 3 tags together whenever you use any one of them.

But we skipped the `<th>` tag that basically stands for `<thead>` as well. The difference? You don't have to use `<th>` tag in combination with any other table-related tag. However, it is usually used to replace `<td>` tags individually to apply a header "look" to a cell.

Applying it to a table will style the `<th>` cell as if it was a header. In other words:

1 `<th>` tag will align text to the center
2 `<th>` tag makes its content bold

94

The `<td>` tag should probably only be used in the context of a header. But here just to demonstrate its versatility, I applied it to all cells within the first row, and one cell in the third column on row 3:

Position	Album	Artist
1	Dark Side of the Moon	Pink Floyd
2	Sgt. Pepper's Lonely Hearts Club Band	The Beatles
3	Led Zeppelin IV (aka ZOSO)	**Led Zeppelin**
4	Abbey Road	The Beatles

Figure 89:

Notice that because our previous CSS was applied only to `<td>` tags, the font family in `<th>` tag as shown in the example above did not inherit Arial font. It's still the default Times New Roman.

But that can also be quickly corrected by adding th to previously written CSS:

```
1  <style type="text/css">
2      table td,
3      table th
4      {
5          font-family: Arial;
6          font-size: 12px;
7          padding: 4px;
8      }
9  </style>
```

Remember to insert this CSS block nested somewhere within the `<head>` tags in your HTML document or inside `<body>` tags, in which case you would also want to add `scoped` property to style tag. Alternatively, you can remove the style tags from this example, and simply enter its contents to a separate "external" CSS file (for example `style.css`) and include it in your document using `<link href = "style.css">` tag within `<head>` tags.

Don't worry if you don't fully understand CSS syntax yet. We'll explore CSS in much greater detail in a future chapter of this book. But it would be difficult to talk about HTML alone in any depth, without bringing up CSS. So far, we're making great progress and we'll go through those subjects later in the book as we continue putting pieces of the puzzle together to form the full picture.

8   Chapter VIII - Forms

HTML forms provide an interface for taking user input. Input elements can manifest themselves as following HTML controls:

- **Text Input** fields for taking username or any similar text-based inputs.

- **Password Input** is a field with all letters replaced by star (*) characters.

- **Clickable Buttons** that provide custom function, for example "Calculate Result."

- **Check Boxes** for creating a single "Yes" or "No" choice.

- **Radio Buttons** for creating a multiple choice selection.

- Usually one **Submit Button** is created at the bottom of the form for sending all form data to another HTML page or an external script for further processing. For example, user-entered data can be sent for permanent storage in a database via a script written in another language, such as PHP or server-side JavaScript.

Note that the HTML form can pass on information entered into it to scripts written in any language. It's up to the web developer to implement that part separately. In this chapter we will only explore creation of the form controls.

8.1   Creating Your First Form

Creating an HTML form is quite simple. And although most forms you will find today are modified by custom CSS to match the overall theme of the website, the HTML code is trivial.

Forms are collections of input elements enclosed by `<form>` and `</form>` tags. Forms usually have a single submit button that sends all of the form input for processing to a script page.

```
1  <form action = "http://example.com/thankyou.php" method = "
      POST">
2
3      <p>First name:</p>
4      <input type = "text" name = "first" value = "" />
5
6      <p>Last name:</p>
7      <input type = "text" name = "last" value = "" />
8
9  <!-- submit this form to "action" script //-->
10      <input type = "submit" value = "Update_Record" />
11
12  </form>
```

This form contains two `<input>` elements and one submit button.

Both input elements contain 3 attributes described below:

- **type** specifies text input type where "text" stands for plain text input.

- **name** is the unique name of this input field.

- **value** is the default value of this input field (can be empty.)

I intentionally skipped placeholder attribute from the source code for clarity. But it's possible that you may want to use it in your own forms.

- **placeholder** attribute provides a hint value for the form's viewer that appears only when text field is empty to provide a clue for what type of information this text field expects.

And finally, this is what the form we just created would look like in the Chrome browser:

Figure 90: A basic HTML form with just two text inputs and a submit button.

The `type` attribute of input fields will physically change the appearance of the control. And beside standard text input, there exist various other elements that can be used to decorate our form with controls that ask the visitor enter all kinds of details.

To name just a few, the type can be `text`, `password`, `radio`, `checkbox` or `submit` all of which would create a different type of user input control. In one of the next section of the book 1.3 Creating Realistic HTML Forms we will take a look at all possible combinations.

Note that the submit button is created using the `<input type = "submit">` tag. Setting its type attribute to `"submit"` ensures that when the button is pressed the browser will send form data to the URL specified in `action` attribute of the `<form>` tag itself.

In the case of our example the submit button will alert the browser for the data to be sent to the imaginary URL at `http://example.com/thankyou.php` assuming that `thankyou.php` script exists at that location.

8.2 Submitting Forms

In our first form example we've taken a look at how the `action` attribute tells the form to which page the information will be sent. It can refer to a "Thank You" page, or a similar page where your website lets the user know that information has been received.

But there is a little more to the process than it seems.

8.2.1 What Are HTTP Requests?

Here we need to briefly mention the concept of an HTTP request. Whenever an HTML page loads into the browser, it is usually a result of an HTTP request. Whatever you enter into address bar is the location of the URL you wish to access. The browser sends a request to that location in order to retrieve the HTML document.

Although the very page that your form is on was initiated by an HTTP request, the form's submit button itself will also initiate one, but this time, to the URL location specified as a value in its `action` attribute. The difference is that the form will actually pass data to that page as well, which is different from simply typing it into your browser's Address Bar.

Both name and the value pair of each element will be submitted to the target page as part of the HTTP request.

8.2.2 GET Method

When you specify GET as a value of the `method` attribute on the `<form>` tag , all of the data will be converted to a string, and sent as part of the URL itself. This way, you can submit the form without even being on the website, by simply typing the parameters into the URL itself.

GET requests are the simplest ones to understand. We'll take a look at how they actually send the information over to a Thank You page in just a moment.

And if your target script specified in `action` attribute of the form allows it, it will read that data from the GET array it receives. Arrays are objects that contain a set of multiple properties.

8.2.3 POST Method

When using POST method, the form does not append data to the URL. Instead, values will be hidden and contained within the request's data payload itself. It will be visible only to the script page specified in action attribute of the form by reading it from a POST array.

The POST method is recommended as the more secure one for submitting form data. That's because it will not be exposed in the address bar as part of the URL. However, this does not fully prevent data from being intercepted either.

Simply using a POST method is not enough to create adequate security for your site. For this reason, when building advanced web applications that require a reasonable degree of security, you will be usually dealing with something called OAuth 2.0 and either REST or GraphQL. But these subjects are way outside of the scope of this book.

Don't get this wrong, none of this actually prevents us from experimenting with HTML forms and passing data to a target page! I just wanted to briefly mention it here, in case you're interested in further exploring the subject of web development.

8.3 HTML Form Controls

We've briefly taken a look at the logic of HTML forms. In this section, you will be introduced to an example of an HTML form for inputting various types of information represented by different HTML controls.

The example in this section can be used as a reference for using most common HTML input controls, such as text input, radio boxes, drop-down menus and so on.

Once our form is constructed, we will also verify user input before it's submitted to the processing script, written in PHP language. Do not worry if you don't know PHP for now, it is a very simple example. This script called submitted.php will be provided as an example only, to demonstrate how an HTML page can send user input for further processing by your website or web application. Advanced PHP scripting is outside the scope of this book, however. It is recommended that you get a separate book for that!

The HTML source code for creating a basic form from is listed below. Note that here, HTML is formatted to match the book format for clarity, and element's attributes are aligned one under the other. However, in your HTML document you can format the HTML code in any way you wish.

```
1   <body>
2
3   <!-- Change cursor arrow to hand pointer when hovering on
         label HTML elements //-->
4   <style type="text/css">label { cursor: pointer; }</style>
5
6   <!-- Begin HTML form by opening the form tag //-->
7   <form action = "submitted.php" method = "POST">
8
9      <b>Enter basic information:</b><br/>
10
11     <input type = "hidden"
12          name = "secret_token"
13          value = "75" />
14
15     Email Address<br />
16     <input type = "text"
17             name = "email"
18     placeholder = "Enter_your_email_address" /><br />
19
20     First Name<br />
21     <input type = "text"
22             name = "firstname"
23     placeholder = "Enter_your_first_name" /><br />
24
25     Last Name<br />
26     <input type = "text"
27             name = "lastname"
28     placeholder = "Enter_your_last_name" /><br />
29
30     Age<br />
31     <input type = "number"
32             name = "age"
33     placeholder = "Enter_your_age" /><br />
34
35     Year of Birth<br />
36     <input type = "number"
37             name = "year"
```

101

```
38      placeholder = "Enter_year_of_birth"
39              min = "1997"
40              max = "2025" /><br />
41
42      Password<br />
43      <input type = "password"
44              name = "password"
45      placeholder = "Enter_your_password" /><br />
46
47      <hr />
48
49      <b>Choose one car make:</b><br/>
50
51      <input id = "aston_martin"
52          type = "radio"
53          name = "car_make" />
54      <label for = "aston_martin">Aston Martin</label>
55      <br/>
56
57      <input id = "ferrari"
58          type = "radio" name = "car_make" CHECKED />
59      <label for = "ferrari">Ferrari</label>
60      <br/>
61
62      <input id = "porsche"
63          type = "radio" name = "car_make" />
64      <label for = "porsche">Porsche</label>
65      <br/>
66
67      <input id = "corvette"
68          type = "radio" name = "car_make" />
69      <label for = "corvette">Corvette</label>
70      <br/>
71
72      <hr />
73
74      <b>Select all that apply:</b><br/>
75
```

```
76    <input id = "driving"
77          type = "checkbox"
78          name = "driving" CHECKED />
79    <label for = "driving" checked>Driving</label>
80    <br/>
81
82    <input id = "crawling"
83          type = "checkbox"
84          name = "crawling" />
85    <label for = "crawling">Crawling</label>
86    <br/>
87
88    <input id = "flying"
89          type = "checkbox" name = "flying" />
90    <label for = "flying">Flying</label>
91    <br/>
92
93    <input id = "swimming"
94          type = "checkbox" name = "swimming" />
95    <label for = "swimming">Swimming</label>
96    <br/>
97
98    <input id = "diving"
99          type = "checkbox" name = "diving" />
100   <label for = "diving">Diving</label>
101   <br/>
102
103   <hr />
104
105   <b>Select favorite fruit:</b><br/>
106
107   <select name = "favorite_fruit">
108     <option value = "apple">Apple</option>
109     <option value = "orange">Orange</option>
110     <option value = "banana">Banana</option>
111     <option value = "strawberry">Strawberry</option>
112     <option value = "peach">Peach</option>
113     <option value = "lemon">Lemon</option>
```

```
114        <option value = "grape">Grape</option>
115      </select>
116
117      <hr />
118
119      <!-- Clicking on this "submit" button will send form's
              data to script specified by the form's action attribute
              //-->
120      <input type = "submit" value = "Submit_This_Form" />
121
122  <!-- Finally, we now need to close the form element //-->
123  </form>
124
125  </body>
```

This code will produce the output shown in Figure 10, when viewed in a web browser.

So what's going on here? We have created several input elements of different types. In HTML, you can change the input controls by modifying the value of the `type` attribute of an `<input>` tag.

For example:

```
1    <!-- Create plain text input //-->
2    <input type = "text" />
3
4    <!-- Replace entered letters with star (*) character //-->
5    <input type = "password" />
6
7    <!-- Create a clickable checkbox //-->
8    <input type = "checkbox" />
9
10   <!-- Create a radio button option //-->
11   <input type = "radio" />
12
13   <!-- Create a hidden value //-->
14   <input type = "hidden" value = "1" />
```

These attributes are pretty basic and easy to remember. They will render

104

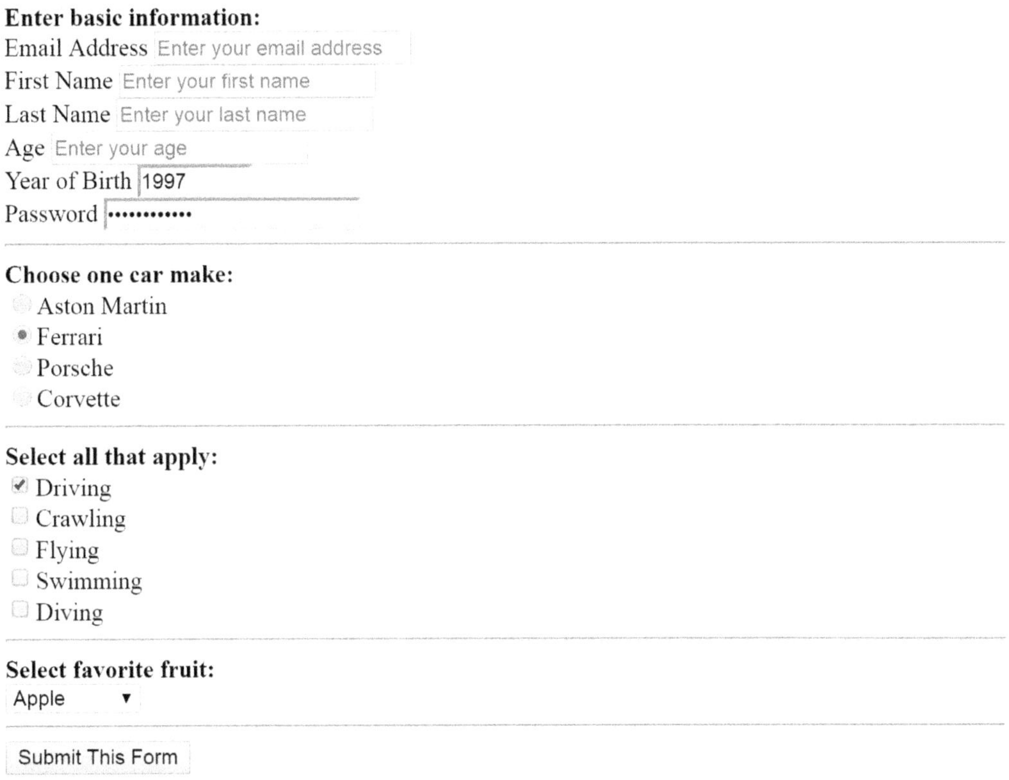

Enter basic information:
Email Address Enter your email address
First Name Enter your first name
Last Name Enter your last name
Age Enter your age
Year of Birth 1997
Password ••••••••••

Choose one car make:
○ Aston Martin
◉ Ferrari
○ Porsche
○ Corvette

Select all that apply:
☑ Driving
☐ Crawling
☐ Flying
☐ Swimming
☐ Diving

Select favorite fruit:
Apple ▼

Submit This Form

Figure 91: A form asking to enter visitor's email address, first and last names, password and a few options.

different types of clickable HTML elements, determined by the needs of your form.

Note that the last type of the input type shown here is a "hidden" value of 1.

8.4   Hidden Form Inputs

Hidden inputs will not visually show up on the form itself. It's for passing custom strings of text or numeric values to the form's target script. The value is usually determined dynamically by JavaScript. It can contain a secret code, a token ID of some sorts, or any other custom information that you wish to send via the form, but don't necessarily require the user to choose or modify it.

8.5 Radio Buttons

Radio buttons behave in a special way by giving the visitor one choice from the same group of answers. To give user a chance to select their favorite car make, for example, you could create a group of choices united by radio button group name. This name is specified under the "name" attribute for each radio button:

```
1  <input type = "radio" name = "car_make" value = "Aston␣
      Martin" />
2  <input type = "radio" name = "car_make" value = "Ferrari" />
3  <input type = "radio" name = "car_make" value = "Porsche" />
4  <input type = "radio" name = "car_make" value = "Chevrolet"
      />
```

This will render just the clickable radio buttons.

8.5.1 Labeling Radio Buttons

You can further decorate them by adding additional text to the right of each radio button. Usually this text is provided by using an HTML tag created specifically for this purpose called label:

```
1  <input type = "radio"
2         name = "car_make"
3        value = "Ferrari"
4           id = "ferrari_id" />
5  <label for = "ferrari_id"> Click to choose Ferrari</label>
```

The label is associated to the id of a radio button by specifying it as a value in its for attribute. Here, it is ferrari_id. Once this link between the label and the radio button is established, clicking on the label will produce the same effect as clicking on the radio button itself. Doing this improves user experience when presented with a selection consisting of more than one radio button.

8.5.2 Determining Default Radio Button

By assigning `CHECKED` property to a radio button element, HTML will display it as the default choice once the web page finished loading in your browser.

```
1  <input type = "radio" name = "car_make" value = "Aston␣
       Martin" />
2  <input type = "radio"
3          name = "car_make"
4         value = "Ferrari" CHECKED />
5  <input type = "radio" name = "car_make" value = "Porsche" />
6  <input type = "radio" name = "car_make" value = "Chevrolet"
       />
```

Leaving a selection consisting of several radio buttons without a default checked value is usually not a good idea.

8.6 Checking Form's Values Before Submitting Them

So far, we've built a very basic HTML form. It doesn't even check whether the values that were entered by the user could be considered as acceptable.

Clicking on the `update record` submit button will send the browser to `action` URL and if no data was entered the default values will be used. The form will be submitted regardless of whether data was entered into the form at all.

The problem? Even blank values may be sent to the server, but this behavior is usually not intended. For example, the fields could be an email address required for account creation or a password that still needs to be validated against a second password field.

In our first example we've taken a look at how to send form values to a PHP script. But there is a catch. Online forms on reputable websites take an extra step and ensure that the data was entered correctly *after* the submit button is clicked but *before* the form is actually sent to the next page. If only we could intercept the values before they are sent to the "thank you" PHP script.

This process is also known as *Form Validation*. In next section an example of testing for accurately entered usernames, email addresses and passwords will be provided using HTML5.

8.7   HTML5 Form Validation

Browser form validation didn't exist *out of the box* until HTML5. And you had to provide your own *JavaScript* solution which often meant writing between 50-100 lines of code or more.

Today, just about any common browser supports it via HTML5. To enable it on your form's input elements, all we have to do is add the HTML5 `require` property to the fields we want to validate.

Let's create an HTML5 form where all four fields are required to be validated:

```
1  <form action="/users/signup" method="post">
2      <label for="username">Username</label>
3      <input id="username" type="text" required>
4      <br/>
5      <label for="email">Email</label>
6      <input id="email" type="email" required>
7      <br/>
8      <label for="password">Password</label>
9      <input id="password" type="password" required>
10     <br/>
11     <label for="password2">Repeat Password</label>
12     <input id="password2" type="password" required>
13     <br/>
14     <input type="submit" value="Submit">
15 </form>
```

That's it!

Just an aesthetic add on: to make sure all labels are the same width, let's write this CSS to force a width of *125 pixels* on all `label` tags from the

HTML example above:

```
1       label { display: inline-block; width: 125px }
```

The result is this form:

Username

Email

Password

Repeat Password

Submit

Figure 92: A basic HTML5 form with 4 required fields.

And when you try clicking submit button on this empty form, built-in HTML5 validator will produce this message on the first field:

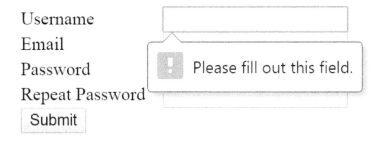

Figure 93: Clicking Submit produces a warning. Username cannot be blank, form is not submitted until this is fixed.

The same goes for all other four fields.

HTML5 can even tell the difference between a *username* and *email address*:

Figure 94: Email address was entered in incorrect format. The HTML5 form's input field with `required` property knows to test for email address because attribute `type` is set to the value of `email`.

The email address requires at least one @ character. HTML5 form will trigger this warning message on empty text input fields with `type = "email"`.

We can take form validation with HTML5 a step further by specifying an exact pattern the user is expected to match.

These patterns are created using yet another language called *Regular Expressions*. Unlike JavaScript that helps us write entire programs, Regular Expressions match patterns.

8.7.1 Regular Expression Patterns

In addition to standard form validation in HTML5 we are able to fine tune how we want to validate each input field based on a pattern.

Traditionally a password must contain only alpha-numeric values, a telephone number must be limited to a number of characters and not contain text... and an email address must contain the "at" character (@).

To verify these requirements a web developer usually writes an additional script in JavaScript language using a built-in object called `RegEx`. But in HTML5, this functionality is provided *out of the box* using the *pattern* attribute.

Let's cover a few examples here. This gives us full control over exactly how we want to validate our input fields.

8.7.2 First and Last Names

You might think this one is easy. All we have to do is check for A through z characters. But upon a closer examination, names come in a variety of formats. And what about those *double-barrelled* names? The ones that contain a *dash*?

Let's take a look:

```
1    Clare O'Connor
2    Martin Luther King, Jr.
3    Mathias d'Arras
4    John-Paul
5    Anne-Marie
```

This regular expression pattern (*that should be provided as the value of the* **pattern** *attribute on any text input field you wish to validate as a first or last name*) will pass most common cases:

```
1   /^[a-z ,.'-]+$/i
```

HTML5 field Example for matching *first and last names*:

```
1   First name:<br/>
2  <input type = "text"
3              id = "first_name"
4           type = "first_name"
5         pattern = "/^[a-z ,.'-]+$/i" required />
6
7   Last name:<br/>
8  <input type = "text"
9              id = "last_name"
10          type = "last_name"
11        pattern = "/^[a-z ,.'-]+$/i" required />
```

8.7.3 Usernames

Usernames are usually alpha-numeric values that can also contain dots and underscores. In this example we also added the dash (-) to the valid character set:

111

```
1   /^[A-z0-9.-_]+$/i
```

HTML5 field Example for matching *usernames*:

```
1   Username:<br/>
2   <input type = "text"
3               id = "username"
4           type = "username"
5       pattern = "/^[A-z0-9.-_]+$/i" required />
```

8.7.4   Email Address

Email addresses are some of the most complex regular expression patterns we must test against when it comes to form validation. It is possible to create a pattern that matches most email addresses, but discards some of the less common (*yet, completely valid*) emails.

If you want to be complete by matching *any email address in existence* with 100% accuracy the following Regular Expression provides a means for validating a *fully RFC 822 compliant regular expression*.

```
1   (?:[a-z0-9!#$%&'*+/=?^_`{|}~-]+(?:\.[a-z0-9!#$%&'*+/=?^_
    `{|}~-]+)*|"(?:[\x01-\x08\x0b\x0c\x0e-\x1f\x21\x23-\x5b\
    x5d-\x7f]|\\[\x01-\x09\x0b\x0c\x0e-\x7f])*")@(?:(?:[a-z0
    -9](?:[a-z0-9-]*[a-z0-9])?\.)+[a-z0-9](?:[a-z0-9-]*[a-z0
    -9])?|\[(?:(?:(2(5[0-5]|[0-4][0-9])
    |1[0-9][0-9]|[1-9]?[0-9]))\.){3}(?:(2(5[0-5]|[0-4][0-9])
    |1[0-9][0-9]|[1-9]?[0-9])|[a-z0-9-]*[a-z0-9]:(?:[\x01-\
    x08\x0b\x0c\x0e-\x1f\x21-\x5a\x53-\x7f]|\\[\x01-\x09\x0b\
    x0c\x0e-\x7f])+)\])
```

Luckily for us, not only do you not have to use this *dinosauruc* pattern – you don't need to.

It's good to keep email validation simple. Just check for presence of @ sign, and a dot:

```
1   /^\S+@\S+\.\S+$/
```

Although this regular expression might pass a few odd cases that are not

112

considered valid email addresses, it is simple and gets the job done for the most part.

HTML5 field Example for matching *email addresses*:

```
1  Email address:<br/>
2  <input type = "email"
3          id = "email"
4        type = "email"
5     pattern = "/^\S+@\S+\.\S+$/" required />
```

8.7.5   Password

Password validation will depend on what you, as the site owner, wish the password patterns to match. Below are listed a few different cases testing for different required conditions of a password string.

The string must contain at least 1 lowercase alphabetical character:

```
1  (?=.*[a−z])
```

The string must contain at least 1 uppercase alphabetical character:

```
1  (?=.*[A−Z])
```

The string must contain at least 1 numeric character:

```
1  (?=.*[0−9])
```

The string must be eight characters or longer:

```
1  (?=.{8,})
```

You can also combine them into one Regular Expression.

And finally... our *password* validation pattern could look this way:

```
1  Username:<br/>
2  <input type = "password"
3          id = "password"
4        type = "password"
5     pattern = "^(?=.*[A−Za−z])(?=.*\d)[A−Za−z\d]{8,}$"
            required />
```

8.7.6 Phone Numbers

Here is a regular expression that will validate most cases:

```
1  ^(\+\d{1,2}\s)?\(?\d{3}\)?[\s.-]\d{3}[\s.-]\d{4}$
```

It matches the following numbers:

```
1    123-456-7890
2    (123) 456-7890
3    123 456 7890
4    123.456.7890
5    +91 (123) 456-7890
```

And our HTML5 would be:

```
1  Phone number:<br/>
2  <input type = "text"
3            id = "phone"
4          type = "phone"
5      pattern = "^(\+\d{1,2}\s)?\(?\d{3}\)?[\s.-]\d{3}[\s.-]\d
          {4}$" required />
```

Regular Expressions are helpful for matching text patterns. But there is no way we can possibly cover the entire scope of *Regular Expressions* in this book.

If you are interested in exploring them further, here is a diagram that provides some very basic examples.

8.7.7　Regular Expressions

Text	Pattern	Return Value (Array)
Remember that time that the trees fell down. The wood crashing through the wall. Remember the sound that could wake the dead. But nobody woke up at all.	/Remember/	["Remember"]
Remember that time that the trees fell down. The wood crashing through the wall. Remember the sound that could wake the dead. But nobody woke up at all.	/Remember/g	["Remember", "Remember"]
Remember that time that the trees fell down. The wood crashing through the wall. Remember the sound that could wake the dead. But nobody woke up at all.	/wall/g	["wall"]
Remember that time that the trees fell down. The wood crashing through the wall. Remember the sound that could wake the dead. But nobody woke up at all.	/[wall]/g	["a", "a", "l", "l", "w", "w", "a"...etc]
Remember that time that the trees fell down. The wood crashing through the wall. Remember the sound that could wake the dead. But nobody woke up at all.	/[.]/g	[".", ".", ".", "."]
Remember that time that the trees fell down. The wood crashing through the wall. Remember the sound that could wake the dead. But nobody woke up at all.	/A-Z/	Only capital letters. A to Z. ["R", "T", "R", "B"]
Remember that time that the trees fell down. The wood crashing through the wall. Remember the sound that could wake the dead. But nobody woke up at all.	/.*/	Match everything until end of line.
Remember that time that the trees fell down. The wood crashing through the wall. Remember the sound that could wake the dead. But nobody woke up at all.	/.*/g	Match everything. Really.

Figure 95: Regular Expression examples.

8.8 Clicking The Submit Button

Our HTML5 form is completed and validated, given user provides some sort of input. But what do we do with the data entered into it?

Forms send the data to another, usually separate script file. That script file can be a "Thank You" page, or some type of confirmation letting the user know that the information has been received.

This file needs to be created separately in your project. Let's just say that for this example, we will create a fresh file and call it `submitted.php`.

Although server-side PHP language is beyond the scope of this book, it is one of the simplest choices made by beginner web developers for solving slightly more advanced programming problems (Because PHP language runs on the server, and not in your browser, it is often used to upload images, work with application data, and processing form input.) Note that for the stated reason, PHP requires some additional set up to work properly locally on your computer.

In other words, it will not work out of the box in your browser (like HTML does,) unless you install Apache server with PHP on your computer first. However, web hosting servers (companies that provide ability to serve your website from a www. location,) have PHP already set up out of the box. If you are eager to start experimenting with more advanced subjects and don't have the time to install Apache on your computer, I recommend getting a web hosting account.

If you're looking to grow in your career as a Web Developer, it is strongly recommended to spend some time learning how to set up a web server to run locally on your PC (or Mac) as this will come up a lot in the future when you move on to advanced web application development. In professional environment if you ever find yourself hired by a software company, this is not only required knowledge but expected as second-nature.

We've chosen PHP as the language for processing our HTML form's submit action. But what does this PHP language look like? Here is a short piece of PHP code (the part of an HTML document wrapped between `<?php ?>` brackets,) that will in fact take the input from our form and display the values that the user entered.

Note also that this script is the one we specified as a value of the `action` attribute in the HTML form: `<form action = "submitted.php">` we created earlier. This is important. The submit button automatically sends the entered form data to this script.

The listing of the script written in PHP language `submitted.php` is saved in the same folder together with your `index.html` file and it contains only four lines of code.

```
1    <html>
2      <head><title>Submitted Form</title>  </head>
3      <pre><?php print_r($_REQUEST); ?></pre>
4    </html>
```

A PHP script can actually be an HTML document! The PHP itself is only embedded into it using PHP brackets. However, nothing is stopping a PHP script from containing only PHP. In fact, some PHP scripts can potentially generate and print HTML tags. For example, when you need content of your HTML page to be dynamically generated.

The difference is that instead of using `.html` file extension, you should save your PHP files using the `.php` file extension. Web servers are usually configured to automatically process `.php` files as PHP scripts. If that isn't the case, PHP code between `<?php ?>` brackets will be rendered as plain text and no PHP code will actually be executed. Properly setting up a PHP server fixes that problem.

When the submit button is clicked, we are sent to this page. This simple PHP script uses a PHP command `print_r`, which in turn prints out the received form data as an object of type Array. Again, you will need to brush up on your PHP scripting in order to fully understand this. But basically, in this case an Array is a collection of property names and values.

The built-in PHP array called `$_REQUEST` will contain form data. Remember how earlier we mentioned that HTML forms send data via something called HTTP requests? That's the purpose of the `$_REQUEST` array. To receive form data. Once the button is clicked, the output of this PHP script is as follows:

```
1  Array
```

117

```
 2  (
 3     [secret_token] => 75
 4     [email] => robert.smith@gmail.com
 5     [firstname] => Robert
 6     [lastname] => Smith
 7     [age] => 24
 8     [year] => 1997
 9     [password] => MyOrangeCat175!
10     [car_make] => on
11     [driving] => on
12     [favorite_fruit] => orange
13  )
```

Notice how our HTML form converted the received values from HTML controls into a neatly organized list that is easy to read. We can now access each value individually from PHP or send it back to JavaScript. What you will do with entered information is up to you.

Note that from the script's point of view, the values entered into password field are no longer blocked by stars. Of course, this is because the server can actually see all received values.

Normally, email and password combinations are used to create log in forms. The PHP script receives the email and password values entered by the visitor. Then the email and password are matched with values in the database on your web server, just to check if that user exists. If entered email and password pair match, the user can be considered logged into your website. If you are interested in learning to build this type of functionality for your own websites, I again recommend picking up a PHP book. You can also create similar functionality with server-side JavaScript and libraries such as React.js, Angular.js or Vue.js.

Because we wrapped PHP script with HTML tags <pre>, the array is neatly formatted by line breaks, forming a readable one column of names associated to entered values on the submitted form. Had that not been the case, you would see something like this in the browser:

```
 1  Array ( [secret_token] => 75 [email] => robert.smith@gmail.
        com [firstname] => Robert [lastname] => Smith [age] => 24
          [year] => 1997 [password] => MyOrangeCat175! [car_make]
```

```
=> on [ driving ] => on [ favorite_fruit ] => orange  )
```

It looks a bit more garbled and less readable. But that's just the result of the output produced by the PHP function `print_r`.

It is not uncommon for input in Array format (a list of name and values, also often separated by commas) to be sent and received back and forth between the server and the front-end of your applications developed in HTML and JavaScript. In fact, a special format in JavaScript exists called JSON (JavaScript Object Notation) to help web developers deal with lists of properties.

Forms can represent user sign up boxes, newsletter subscriptions, places where financial information such as credit cards and so on can be entered. What you will do with received data will depend primarily on the purpose of your website or application.

Many online newsletter websites such as Mailchimp and Constant Contact provide HTML and JavaScript code you can simply embed directly into your website. They will take care the server-side part and provide you with a list of email addresses that subscribed to your form. But nothing is stopping you from continuing to explore server-side programming on your own.

8.9   Using Custom Images To Replace Submit Button

If you've ever installed a PayPal donation or payment button on your website, you have installed an HTML form. You may have wondered how the PayPal flavor of HTML form makes their orange buttons appear on the page, instead of the generic gray (or transparent on Mac operating systems) HTML button:

Figure 96: Custom PayPal HTML form button. How was it made?

When you specify type of an input element as `image` then HTML will interpret it as a submit button. But additionally, it will look for the actual image you wish to use as the submit button! Image must be specified as URL using secondary `src` (or alternatively, `source`) attribute as in `<input type = "image" src = "my-image.png" />`. Here is an example of what it would look like in HTML source code:

```
1  <form>
2    <!-- create several input elements here ... //-->
3    <input type = "text" /> <!-- etc. //-->
4
5    <!-- Within <form> elements, input of type "image" will
6         automatically function like a submit button //-->
7    <input type = "image" src = "my-submit-button.png" />
8  </form>
```

In this case `my-submit-button.png` is the filename of the custom image that replaces the submit button in your form. And even though theoretically this should work, it can probably be considered a slightly outdated way of styling a submit button.

In modern web development, the style of a submit button is usually specified using external CSS and not an input element of type "image". That attribute is a relic from the old days, before CSS had the capacity to change the look and feel of a form button.

I don't want to spend time talking about features that are slowly becoming deprecated in HTML. But I wanted to mention type=image submit buttons as one of the many examples where outdated features still work in modern browsers. The lesson here is, just because something works, it doesn't mean that it should be used, if you wish to follow modern development standards. And there are quite a few of these features!

When we get to later chapters of the book, you will see that CSS is the ideal way of styling all of your HTML elements. HTML provides only the structure of your layout.

9 Chapter IX: Thinking In Pixels

9.1 Position and Size of HTML Elements

We covered several types of HTML elements and what they appear like in the browser when you hit refresh. But HTML also gives us control over the *position* and *size* of elements on the screen.

Up until this point in the book we thought of HTML element positioning as arbitrary. In order to get a good grasp on controlling our element's position and size with a lot more precision we need to start *thinking in pixels*.

Having control over position of an element provides flexibility. They allow for more freedom of expression when it comes to website style. Because HTML is closely related to graphic design, when positioning your elements you will be asking questions like: "Should this element be located 4 or 8 pixels away from the left side of the screen?" or "How does increasing height of a button by 5 pixels contributes to overall look & feel of my layout?"

9.2 What Are Pixels?

A `pixel` is the single unit of space used for measuring distance between text and other HTML elements. Getting close enough to the computer screen you'll notice that pretty much everything you are seeing on it is constructed from tiny squares. Each one of those square boxes is a pixel.

A pixel is simply the tiniest square dot on the screen! Pixels also have a color value created from three channels: Red, Green and Blue. HTML allows us to set color to any element using hexadecimal numbering system. We'll take a look at color shortly. For now just know that pixels can be located at a precise position on the screen.

Let's demonstrate how if we zoom in close enough, we can see that letters are actually made up of pixels.

Thinking about HTML elements on this microscopic level is important because User Interface wire-frames created by graphic designers are usually to be followed with "pixel-perfect" precision. And who can blame them? Hallmark of

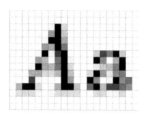

Figure 97: Zooming in on text displayed in your HTML document reveals that text and other HTML elements actually consist of pixels.

good design is caring about every pixel on the screen.

9.3 Position

In the context of creating websites you will be often dealing with pixels to set *location* and *size* of HTML elements.

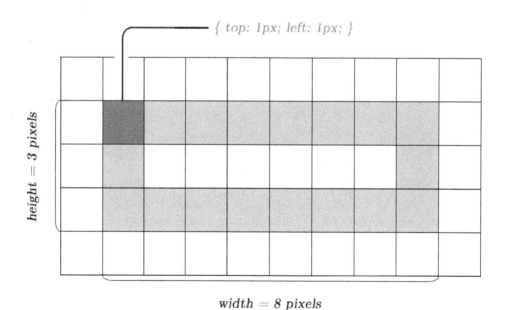

{ top: 1px; left: 1px; }

height = 3 pixels

width = 8 pixels

Figure 98: An area with dimensions of 10 x 5 and a 8 x 3 box inside, measured in pixels.

Website layouts are constructed to adapt to a large variety of devices. For example a standard monitor can go up to 1920 x 1080 to fill the entire screen. One of the latest Amazon Kindle Fire devices spans across 1200 x 1920 and an Apple iPad Pro can reach up to 2048 x 2732 screen resolution in pixels. A 4K monitor has a resolution of 4096 x 2304.

Your website or web application will deal with smaller resolutions. This is because your website is assumed to appear within the boundaries of a browser which can be resized by the user.

In addition, traditional website layouts are often "centered" vertically on the screen and consist of multiple, smaller blocks making up the entire layout. This avoids situations where your website is viewed on a very large screen. If its layout is set to 100% of the screen's width, its design may disintegrate and no longer appear natural.

9.4   Hierarchies of Coordinate Systems

All HTML elements we create are usually located somewhere within other elements.

This means that each HTML element contains its own local coordinate system.

For example, if you wish to position a child element within a parent element already located somewhere in your HTML document, the child will inherit parent's coordinate system which takes origin in the upper left corner of the parent element.

This can be further demonstrated by this minimalistic diagram shown in Figure 9. Note that upper left corner is at 0 x 0, not 1 x 1.

When designing your own HTML layouts you will often start with thinking about the upper left corner of an element first. You can calculate the position of any child element within it with pixel-precision using this corner as a starting point. This is why it's often referred to as element's *relative* position.

Elements within other elements inherit relative positioning to one another by default.

If you need a certain element to appear at a precise location within another

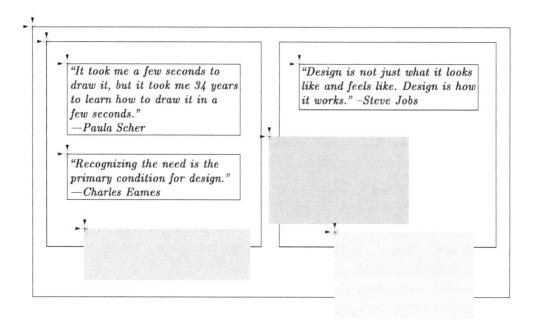

Figure 99: Arrange elements on the screen any way you wish. The sky is the limit.

element you will change **position** property from its default value of **relative** to **absolute** and provide pixel location using two additional CSS properties **top** and **left**. If neither top nor left values are provided **position:absolute;** will be ignored by HTML.

In CSS the upper left corner is defined as {**left:0px; right:0px**}. You can further reduce it to {**left:0; right:0;**}. Note, however, you are required to append **px** to *non*-0 positioning and size values, whereas {**left:32;**} is illegal and {**left:32px;**} should be used instead. But {**left:0;**} is acceptable.

This is only because **px** unit – while the most common – is not the only way to specify size or position of an element. When it comes to font size, it can also be specified in **em** units instead of **px**.

Originally, **em** in typography stood for the width of the capital letter M.

124

This was true for traditional printing before the Internet. This is because M was the type of a character that could fit into a square box. These so called *em-quads* or *mutton-quads* were used by the first printing press. Johann Gutenberg holds the distinction of being the inventor of the movable-type printing press. In 1455, Gutenberg produced what is considered to be the first book ever printed: a Latin language Bible, printed in Mainz, Germany. A town that by incident also starts with letter M!

As far as HTML is concerned, an `em` is a single unit equal to the currently specified point size. Therefore if font-size of the document is 12pt, then 1em is equal 12pt. Size specified in em units is scalable. If current point size is 12pt then 2em would equal 24pt. Likewise, a fractional .5em would equal 6pt.

9.5   Position & Display Properties

Using intuitive diagrams below we'll quickly go over CSS properties `position` and `display` which give us ability to modify element's default behavior.

We'll start with simple text spans, but by modifying these properties on just about any other element will produce the same or similar behavior.

9.6   Text Spans

The examples below demonstrate basic idea behind how HTML thinks of relative positioning of simple elements. Since we know that `<body>` is a required tag in any HTML document, we will assume that elements in these examples are nested within it (or a similar parent element, such as `<div>`, etc).

That makes it easy to see that every element will be placed within another element, usually referred to as its parent. The element itself then becomes its child.

To demonstrate default text position behavior, we'll assume that most examples will be based around some text entered between `<span>`*here*`<span>` tags.

top

left

automatic height

automatic
width

top and **left** are automatically calculated
when element's display style is inline
or inline-block to accommodate for
continuous text display.

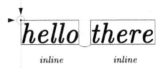

inline   inline

The inline display style is applied by default to
all HTML's elements of type <span>. Regular
text can be used in between spans as well. Here,
there is a single space between two <span> tags.

The example on the left is this simple HTML. Note that HTML automatically calculates width of text spans, depending on length of text.

```
1   <body>
2       <span>hello</span>
3   </body>
```

Example to the right was generated using following code:

```
1   <body>
2       <span>hello</span> <span>there</span>
3   </body>
```

Here we've used **<span>** tags only as an example, but they're great for modifying appearance of words or phrases that go beyond italic or bold text that can be imitated with **<b>** and **<i>** tags. For example, you can highlight a single word or a phrase within a sentence by applying CSS via element's **style** attribute:

```
1   <body>
2       "The only <span style = "background: black; color: white
           ;">difference </span> between me and a madman is that
           I'm not mad." − Salvador Dali (1904−1989)
3   </body>
```

This HTML code will produce the output shown in Figure 11.

Here, we've changed the background color of the word *difference* to black and set its font color to white.

126

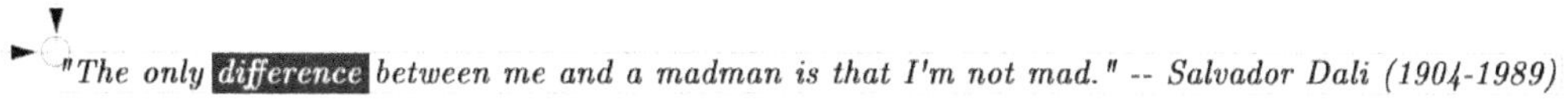

"The only difference between me and a madman is that I'm not mad." -- *Salvador Dali (1904-1989)*

Figure 100: A quote by Salvador Dali, spanish Surrealist painter.

9.7 Default CSS Properties

Remember that all HTML tags have default CSS style settings even if none are provided by you. By default the `<span>`'s CSS property `display` is set to value of: `inline`. This is why no matter how many span tags there are, they will always appear *inline* or in other words in *"one immediately after the other"* order producing a continuous string of text.

But this default behavior can be modified. And although isolated cases like this one may not make a lot of sense right now, the situation in which changing default properties of an element becomes useful is based on the specific behavior you're trying to achieve when designing your own layouts.

9.8 From Inline to Block

Let's set the `display` property of the `<span>` tag to `block` and see how it affects the element.

Figure 101: Changing a display property of a text span from "inline" to "block".

127

Overriding `display:inline` with `display:block` has extended the element's width all the way down to the right margin of the parent element!

In other words, this means that this element will "block" all other elements to its right, effectively "bumping" them down underneath it.

Moreover, any elements that follow with `display:inline` (or any other display property, for that matter) will now appear just below the blocking element.

9.9 Top, left, bottom, right

In addition to `top` and `left` properties, elements with {`position:absolute`} may also specify their position using `bottom` and `right` properties. You might already guess what they do. Let's take a look at this drawing to demonstrate it.

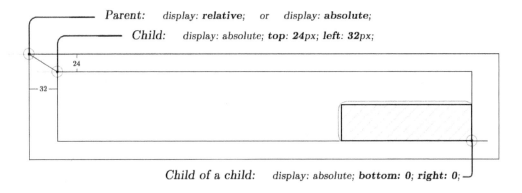

Figure 102: The innermost child is positioned at the right bottom corner using `bottom` and `right` properties. These values can also be negative! Which, in this case would push the innermost child outside its parent.

The property `top` cannot be used together with property `bottom`. Likewise, `left` cannot be used with `right` at the same time.

Another lesson learned here is that some relative elements will appear within absolute elements, and the other way around. But there is one HTML rule that might throw you off guard at first. If an absolute element is specified within an element whose display type is missing or unset, then the child element within it that has absolute position will be relative to the upper left corner *of the screen itself* (or the *root element* in the whole parental hierarchy) and not its direct parent!

For this reason to maintain good control over where you wish your elements to appear, always remember to specify display as either `relative` or `absolute`.

In fact sometimes the CSS star directive is used to set relative position to all elements on the screen * {`display:relative;`}.

We're slowly moving toward elements using absolute positioning. While we're on the subject let's take a look at one more example where we will specify both *position* and *size* of an element and see how it sometimes affects its children elements.

9.10   HTML Element Size

Size of elements is determined by CSS properties `width` and `height`. It's really that simple. Just add them to CSS describing your element:

```
1  <body>
2    <div style = 'position: absolute;
3                         top: 24px;
4                        left: 32px;
5                       width: 100px;
6                      height: 46px;
7                      border: 1px solid black;'>
8       Determine element's width and height.
9    </div>
10 </body>
```

This example will produce a `<div>` element with width=100 and height=50. Additionally there is a 1px solid line border in gray color, just to visualize the new size of the element:

Notice that in this case the text does not fully fit into the box. If the container is too small for the text, it will leap outside of its bounds. It's your responsibility as a designer to make sure this doesn't happen.

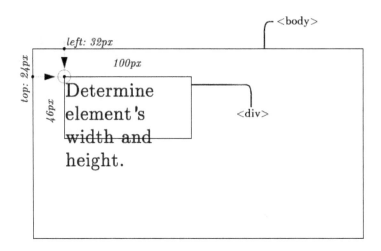

Figure 103: CSS is unforgiving when text area is greater than that of its parent element.

But what if it is your intention to hide overlapping text within a given element? No problem. CSS offers a special property `overflow` to handle this case. Let's apply `overflow:hidden` to this example to see what happens:

```
1  <body>
2    <div style = 'position: absolute;
3                        top: 24px;
4                       left: 32px;
5                      width: 100px;
6                     height: 46px;
7                     border: 1px solid black;
8                   overflow: hidden '>
9       Determine element's width and height.
10   </div>
11 </body>
```

With `overflow:hidden`, the text now cuts off at the element's bounding box:

130

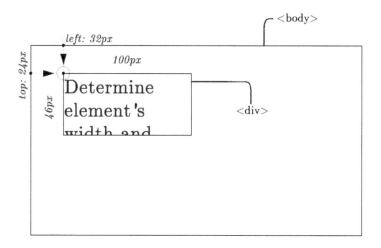

Figure 104: By using `overflow:hidden` CSS property we have effectively restricted children from *visually* escaping the bounding box of the parent element. This works with other HTML elements as well, not just text.

9.11   Margin, Padding and Borders

We've explored position and size of HTML elements. But there are many more default properties to each one of them. Together they help us gain even more control over their appearance and style.

For example properties `padding`, `margin` and `border` can significantly modify visual appearance of an HTML element.

The diagram in Figure 18. explores relationship between the element's size and other properties. You can see here that the element itself can occupy a relatively small area, compared to the area taken up by its padding or margin. In typography using white space around text can help its readability. Using these properties can help you make elements containing text more readable and pleasing to the eye.

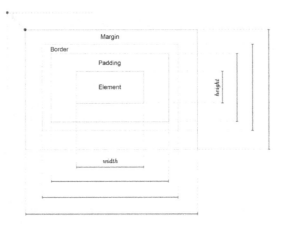

Figure 105: When present, CSS properties `margin`, `borders` and `padding` can make the actual width and height of the element larger than the values specified using the *width* and *height* for that element.

9.11.1 Changing Properties For Individual Sides of Elements

CSS properties `margin`, `border` and `padding` can be specified for each individual side separately. For example, to add a border only to the *left* side of the element, the property `border-left` can be used as follows:

```
1    <div style = 'border-left: 1px solid black;'>Message</div>
```

Similarly, you can apply the border to any other side of the element individually:

With time this can get tedious. So an alternative way of specifying border style to an element was created. You can specify border on any side of the element with just one command. The format is simple:

```
    border: top right bottom left;
```

Where `top`, `right`, `bottom` and `left` is the border thickness in pixels.

But this shorthand format requires that border `style` and `color` are specified separately. If this step is skipped this shorthand will not work. So our CSS therefore is:

132

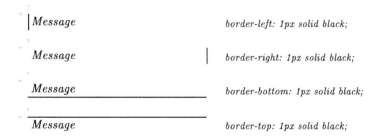

Figure 106: Applying border to any side of the element.

```
border−color:  black;
border−style:  solid;
border:  1px  1px  0  0
```

Finally, HTML code above will produce the following outcome:

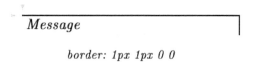

border: 1px 1px 0 0

Figure 107: Shorthand format for borders on two sides of an element at the same time.

Just to be complete, here is how you can set up borders on either top and bottom or left and right sides of an element:

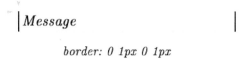

border: 0 1px 0 1px

Figure 108: Setting borders on both sides of the element.

Likewise, to set margin or padding to **10px** only on the left side of an element you can use shorthands **margin:0 0 0 10px** and **padding:0 0 0 10px** properties respectively.

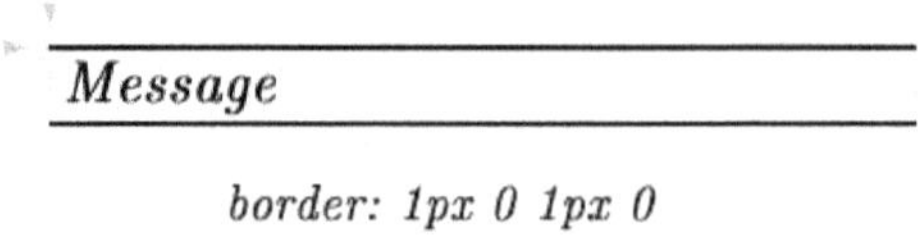

Message

border: 1px 0 1px 0

Figure 109: Display borders only on top and bottom sides of the element.

You can also set these values with `padding-left:10px` or `margin-left:10px`.

10   Chapter X: Text Behavior

In HTML element position is determined by default properties of an HTML tag. For example, a `span` tag is treated as text, therefore it inherits *inline* behavior. A `div` tag is treated is a "blocking" element and is assumed to behave as an element whose display property is set to *block*.

Images are treated as inline *and* blocking at the same time (*inline-block*). It takes some time to play around with all of the CSS properties to learn how default values affect behavior of various elements and what happens when you *override* them with your own.

Iteratively – over a long period of time – you will develop awareness of these special sets of rules that govern element position in HTML. Inevitably, you will also develop your own style of writing HTML and CSS.

Because writing HTML code and layout design are just two different sides of the same coin, many web designers learn about these rules intuitively, by interacting with their own code in the browser.

To accurately visualize what happens in each case, we will add a border around each element, which normally wouldn't appear there. This will give us an idea of how default CSS properties affect element's behavior, dimensions and placement within a parent element.

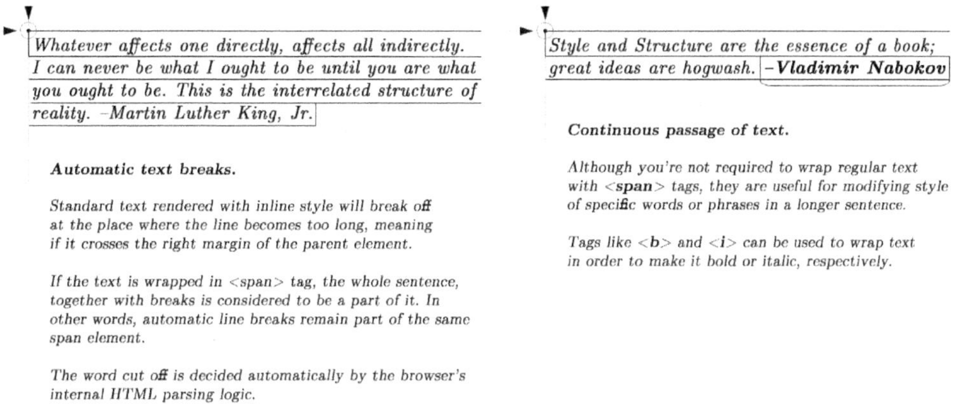

Whatever affects one directly, affects all indirectly. I can never be what I ought to be until you are what you ought to be. This is the interrelated structure of reality. –Martin Luther King, Jr.

Automatic text breaks.

Standard text rendered with inline style will break off at the place where the line becomes too long, meaning if it crosses the right margin of the parent element.

If the text is wrapped in <span> tag, the whole sentence, together with breaks is considered to be a part of it. In other words, automatic line breaks remain part of the same span element.

The word cut off is decided automatically by the browser's internal HTML parsing logic.

*Style and Structure are the essence of a book; great ideas are hogwash. –**Vladimir Nabokov***

Continuous passage of text.

*Although you're not required to wrap regular text with <**span**> tags, they are useful for modifying style of specific words or phrases in a longer sentence.*

*Tags like <**b**> and <**i**> can be used to wrap text in order to make it bold or italic, respectively.*

Figure 110:

10.1   inline

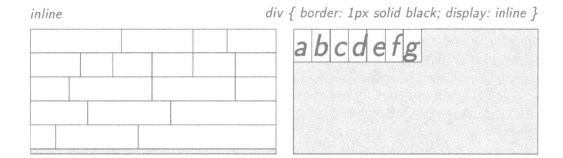

inline

div { border: 1px solid black; display: inline }

Figure 111: Default inline behavior (set as `display: inline`) interprets elements as text. This means that content placed within a series of inline elements will begin at the place where the previous inline element ends.

The `span` element is automatically assumed to behave as an *inline* element. But setting `display: inline` to *any* HTML element will convert it to this form.

10.2   block

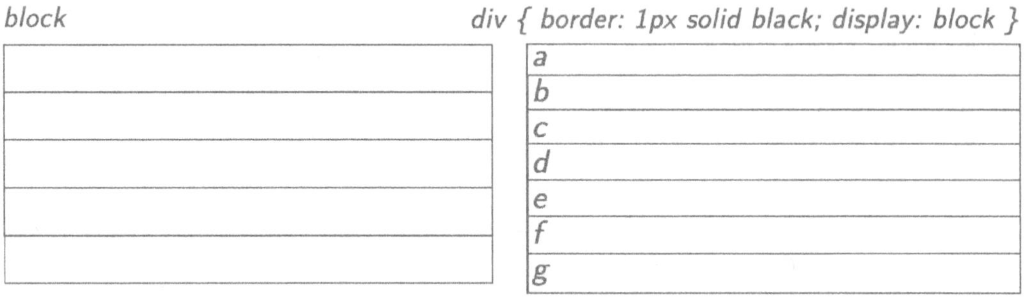

block   div { border: 1px solid black; display: block }

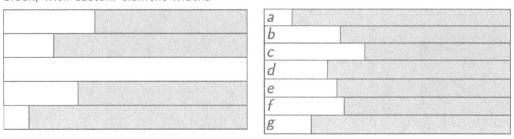

Figure 112: When working with `display: block` it is assumed that the element's *width* will stretch horizontally across the entire width of its *parent element*. In other words, blocking elements will "block" an entire row of space, in contrast to inline elements that abruptly end at the width of the inner content.

Setting width of a blocking element's to something less than its parent's width will continue blocking the rest of the row anyway:

block, with custom element widths

Figure 113: Setting smaller width to blocking elements doesn't modify its blocking behavior. This introduces the concept of separation between element's behavior and its *content area*.

10.3   inline-block

If you need both inline and blocking behavior `inline-block` can be used. Assuming a number of square div elements, following result can be achieved:

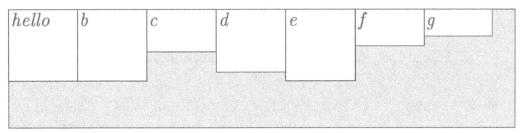

Figure 114: `display:    inline-block;` is like inline, except it allows you to specify element size.

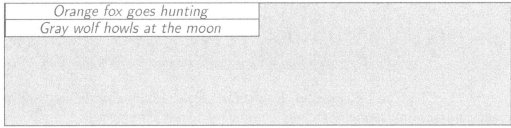

Figure 115: Two elements side by side with `display:    block` and `width: 50%`

The same two elements but now with `display:    inline-block:`

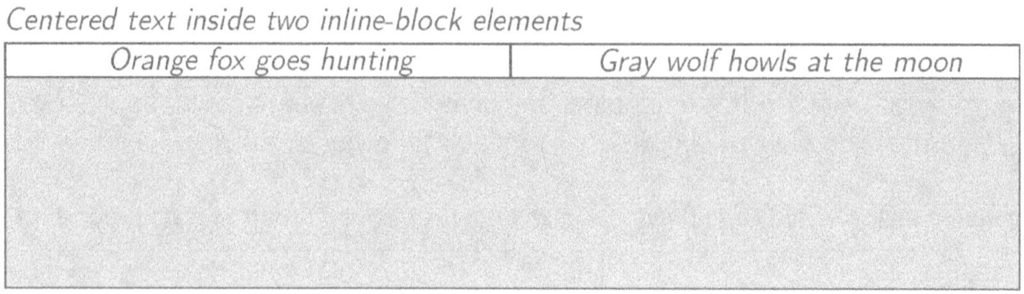

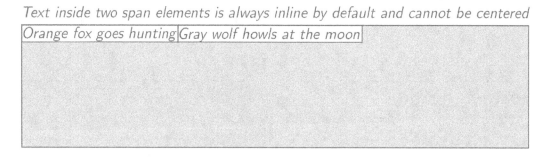

Centered text inside two inline-block elements

| Orange fox goes hunting | Gray wolf howls at the moon |

Figure 116: `display:` `inline-block` and `width:` `50%`

However, centering text within an *inline* element is impossible. Changing the sample above to `display:` `inline` will treat each element as span of text again:

Text inside two span elements is always inline by default and cannot be centered

| Orange fox goes hunting | Gray wolf howls at the moon |

Figure 117: Text inside two span elements is always inline by default and it makes no sense centering it.

In this chapter we've taken a look at basic text behavior within *inline*, *block* and *inline-block* elements.

Once you get a good grasp on how that works, you'll be ready for moving on to slightly more advanced techniques of arranging elements on your HTML page. They will be visualized in the next chapter.

11 Chapter XII: HTML Elements – Common Properties

Every HTML element, *blocking* or *inline* has structural composition that may not be obvious at first – because all properties that deal with size are set to 0 by default.

11.0.1 Anatomy of HTML Elements

In reality, an HTML element consists of *content area, padding,* a *border* and a *margin.*

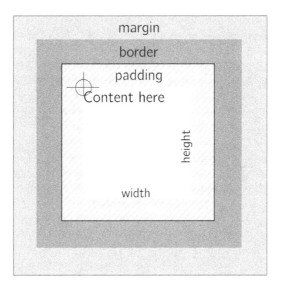

Figure 118: HTML Element Anatomy – structural composition of an HTML element.

Note that the X and Y location of an element (determined by `top` and `left` CSS properties) refers to the upper left corner of the *content area* when padding, border and margin are set to 0.

Changing *padding, border* or *margin* to something greater than its default value of 0 will not automatically change neither its location nor its dimensions (*top* and *left*, *width* and *height* *values of the element.*) even though the element will noticeably be located at a different location on the screen.

How can we then determine the actual width and height of the element in these cases? You can use JavaScript library such as jQuery that provides methods that calculate these values for you. But this is outside of the scope of this book.

Increasing padding value to the element will increase its blocking width, but not the width of its content area. So at times it's difficult to determine as to what should be the element's actual width.

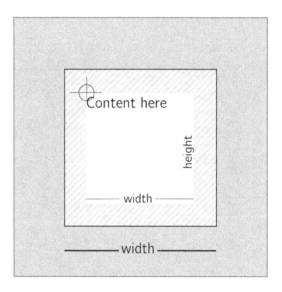

Figure 119:

However, you can retain the padding and suppress this from happening by setting your element's `box-sizing` property to a value of `border-box`:

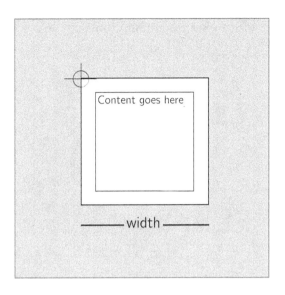

Figure 120: `box-sizing: border-box;`
Notice that the padding now occupies the *inner* area of the element. Now width and height of the element are their original values, and the content is still padded within the element.

Another common thing to do to HTML elements is to max out their rounded corners properties to create a circle using `border-radius` property:

Figure 121: `border-radius: 500px;` (*or set it to actual width of the square element*)

To expand on the previous example, a shadow can be added to create an even more dramatic effect:

Figure 122: `box-shadow:   0 0 10px #0000`

The values of the box-shadow property are explained below:

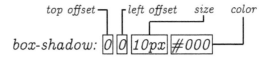

Figure 123: Four values supplied to **box-shadow** property separated by space. Here color black (*hexadecimal #000*) is used to provide the base shadow color.

These techniques are often used for decorating HTML buttons:

Figure 124: Rounded corners and a shadow used to create a Subscribe button with centered text.

Box shadow can be used in creative ways to add *double* (or even *triple*) border effect.

We've taken a look at stacking multiple backgrounds earlier in the book. In the same exact way, providing multiple values to the box-shadow property, it is possible to create multiple borders.

Although doing it this way does not guarantee 100% browser support, since this is literally a hack, and not standard implementation, it's still good to know that this ability exists:

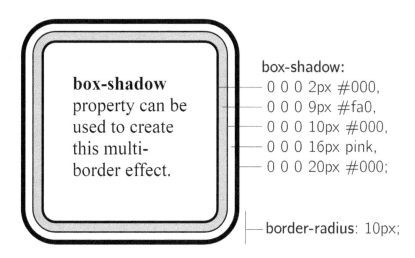

Figure 125: Multiple borders can be used by "hacking" the box-shadow property. Provide each shadow value separated by comma.

In this example the three elements are set to `inline-block`. But in reality, visibility property is independent of the element's display type. The idea is the same – retain the placement of an element but don't draw it.

Thus far we covered a few interesting modifications that can be applied to styling HTML elements. In the next chapter we'll take an even closer look by shifting focus to positioning elements on the screen.

11.0.2 Visibility

Visibility of an HTML element is controlled by `visibility` property.
Possible values are `visible` (*default*) and `hidden`.

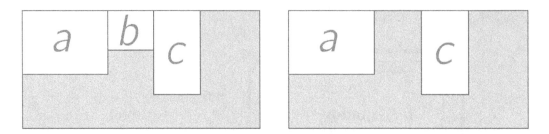

Figure 126: **Left:** Three elements with `visibility:visible` (*default*).
Right: The same three elements, with element b's `visibility` set to `hidden`.

Setting visibility property to `hidden` doesn't actually remove the element from the document. The browser simply skips drawing it. But structurally, it is still part of the document:

11.0.3 Positioning

It is very common to want to position an element exactly at the middle of the screen. This technique is often used to create the main container for the entire website. It's convenient because even if the browser is resized, the element remains automatically aligned to the center.

One way of accomplishing that would be to simply add *automatic margins* to an HTML element whose `display` property is set to `block`:

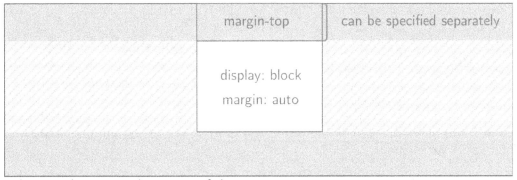

Align an element to the center of the screen using automatic margins

Figure 127: `display:  block; margin:  auto; width:  500px;`

To place an element at an exact location, relative to its parent element `position: absolute` property can be used. It also requires supplying `display:  block` and the actual placement in pixels using `top` and `left` properties:

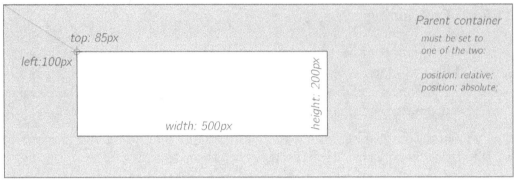

Using absolute placement with position:absolute property

Figure 128: `display:block; position:absolute; top:85px; left:100px; width:500px; height:200px;`

One of my favorite features of CSS when it comes to *absolute* positioning of elements is the ability to define the origin of location, based on any of the four corners of an element.

This is useful when you want to create a placeholder for pop-up notification messages that can potentially appear in any corner of the screen:

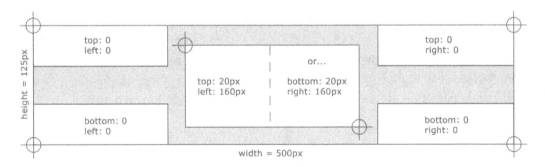

Figure 129: You can use **left**, **right**, **top** and **bottom** properties to change origin of location. But you cannot use **left** together with **right**, or **top** together with bottom on the same element... for obvious reasons.

146

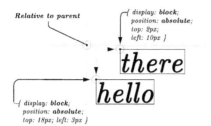

Figure 130: Absolute position applied to HTML elements containing text.

To fix your element on the screen relative to the browser view (*regardless if the horizontal scroll bar changes location*) is often used for creating "overlay" effect. The idea behind it is simple:

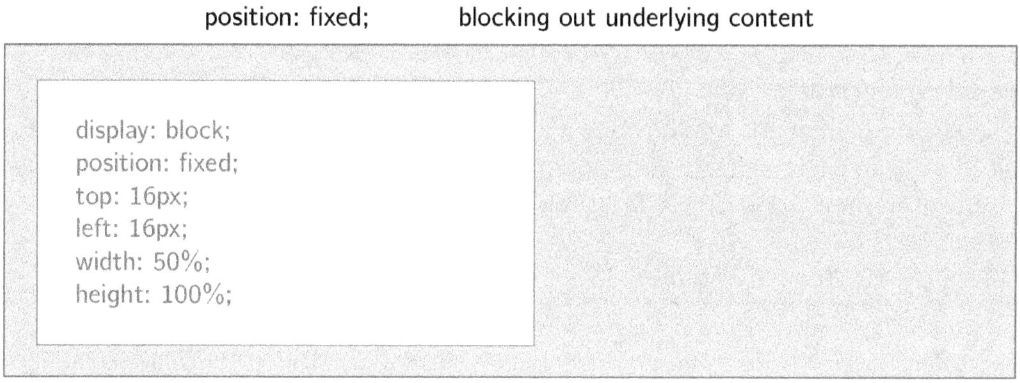

position: fixed;   **blocking out underlying content**

```
display: block;
position: fixed;
top: 16px;
left: 16px;
width: 50%;
height: 100%;
```

Figure 131: `display:block; position:fixed; top:16px; left:16px; width:50%; height:100%;`

Elements "fixed" to the screen can be used to "gray out" the background when you need to display a custom modal dialog box as depicted on the following diagram:

Figure 132: When you post a tweet, the background is shaded out by a full screen element with 50% opacity. The primary user interface controls are then displayed on top of that layer.

11.0.4 Floating Elements

Elements that use relative and absolute position are great for making our life easier when creating various layouts. But there comes a time when you need to "float" an element to make room for other content. Floating elements usually shift to either left or right side, opening up more room for elements specified right after them in your HTML code.

floating elements align naturally along the row, producing a gap between

Figure 133: Two elements with `float:left` behave similar to standard inline text. Another element with `float:right` was added here to demonstrate that content doesn't have to leave the same horizontal area, at the expense of creating a gap if the combined width of all floating elements is shorter than the parent.

Here you have to make a fair judgment based on your layout, as to how you want to handle floating elements. As you will see from the following example, when both floating element's widths combined are greater than the width of their parent container, the second element inherits block-like behavior:

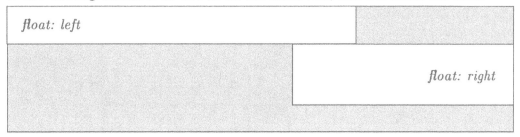

Figure 134: Floating can sometimes be blocking.

But what if you wanted to push a floating element that was set to float in the same direction, onto the next line? You can use `clear:both` directive to accomplish that:

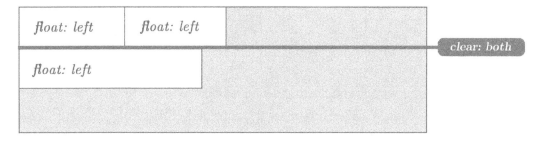

Figure 135: Clearing floating content with `clear:both`.

11.1 Element Modifications

11.1.1 Rounded Corners

Creating rounded corners by changing border-radius property

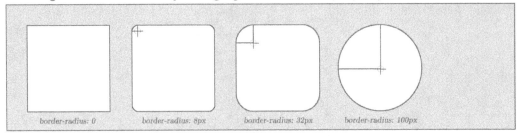

Figure 136: Round corners in a nutshell.

Rounded corners are used to create buttons:

Creating a custom button

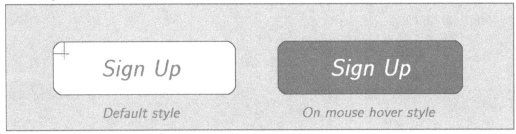

Figure 137: Buttons with rounded corners.

11.1.2 Z-Index

Let's say we mastered HTML element placement on the screen in two dimensions (X and Y.) Still you will encounter cases where you need to pick out some elements to appear "on top" of the others. Even if this isn't how they were listed in your HTML code structure.

The `z-index` property to the rescue. You can bring out any element whose `display` property was set to value of `absolute` and ensure that it is always

150

displayed "above" the rest. In other words, on the Z-axis.

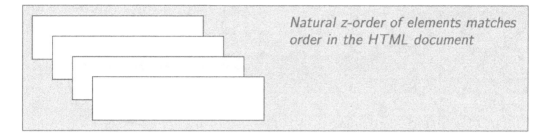

Figure 138: Natural order of elements in HTML document.

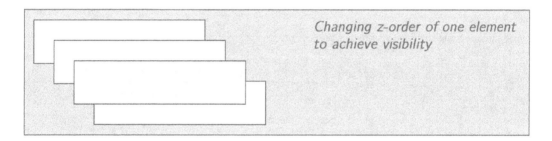

Figure 139: The `z-index` property can bring out elements to the front.

11.1.3 box-shadow

We already covered box shadow earlier. But here are a few more examples.

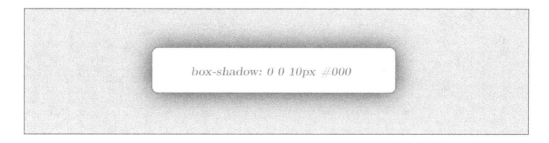

Figure 140: Shadow is centered at the element.

Figure 141: Shadow is displaced by a few pixels from the element to create a *drop-shadow* effect.

And finally... by specifying light colors you can turn a shadow into this glowing effect:

Figure 142: Glowing effect can be simulated by using bright colors with `box-shadow` property.

11.1.4 Scale, Translate, Rotate

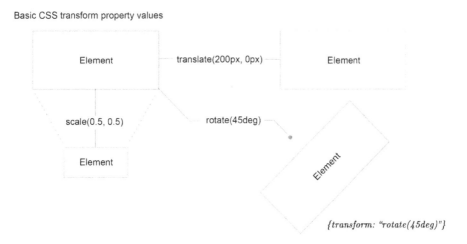
Basic CSS transform property values

Figure 143: Scaling, rotating and translating.

12 Chapter XII: Layout Structure

Aside from creating semantic structure of your document, looking from the vantage point of graphic design, the very purpose of HTML code is to provide *structure. This cannot be stressed enough.* Structural composition is all around us. We see it in automobiles, airplanes, large high-rise buildings or even a country road barn!

Structure cannot be avoided if your plan is to create meaningful user experience. This is why it's important to spend some time mapping out the structure of your creation on a piece of paper before even writing a single line of HTML code. Thinking in terms of structure makes your design easier to adapt to new circumstance in the future.

Structure is why blogs look like blogs – continuous blocks of text stories with a smaller box at the bottom to leave a comment after reading. Your car (*if you have one*) is designed with particular structure in mind. The front door is right by the seat and the steering wheel. The wheels balance the vehicle on the ground. It may be different medium, but the principle is the same.

Think of what your website is trying to accomplish and choose to build a proper layout around that intent. By combining various CSS style properties, you will use common sense and your innate graphic design talent to build out initial wireframe. Then, by using various HTML elements and CSS styles discussed in this book (*and based on your own experiments*) you will arrange them to create a layout that matches your creative vision.

— — —

Up to this point we've covered enough to get us started on the journey to building your own web application layouts. At least, their initial basic structure. Practice and experiment. And remember...this – or any other – book should serve only as a starting point! It cannot replace actual experience writing code.

12.1   Flex

Flex or "flex box" (*also known as CSS Flexible Box*) is a way of arranging your HTML elements in a way that automatically adjusts across a given span of space – the arbitrary page width in the browser – for example.

Flex was also created to make it easier to create layouts consisting of columns and rows for various situations. Two of which are depicted on following diagrams:

Figure 144: A possible HTML layout that can be constructed using CSS flex properties.

Figure 145: Another layout that can be efficiently solved using CSS flex properties.

Flex cells whose **flex-wrap** property is set to the value of **wrap** will automatically adapt to the current browser's dimensions. Consider this example of the same exact layout being viewed in an increasingly narrowing browser window:

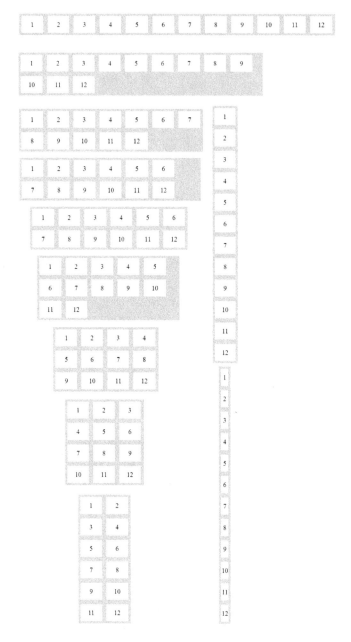

Figure 146: flex-wrap: wrap

I wish we could talk more about flex in this book. Because it's such a neat system of aligning HTML elements to the parent window with unknown dimensions. But we cannot dedicate too much space to CSS specification in this book. My suggestion is to find a good flex tutorial online.

12.2 Grid

Because this is not primarily a CSS book we cannot spend much time talking about CSS grid – a fairly recent addition to the CSS language (*it is 2018 as of the writing of this book.*) However, it helps to know it exists, because it is already gaining popularity among web designers.

Unlike other layout-creation strategies (*floating* and *flex* for instance) the CSS grid provides an intuitive way of arranging your HTML elements by dividing them into cells.

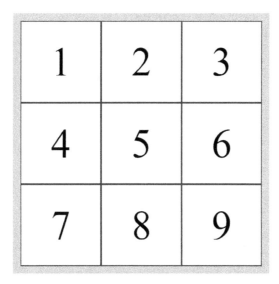

Figure 147: CSS grid with parent container set to **grid-template-columns:** `auto auto auto`

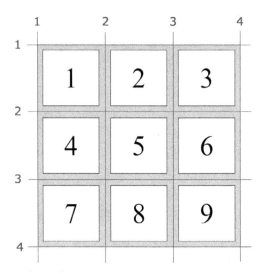

Figure 148: Unlike functionality provided by any of the other CSS properties, CSS grid is mindful of *numbering spaces in between the cells*. This is useful for providing *start* and *end* lines, when you want to stretch a container across multiple cells, as will be shown in the next example.

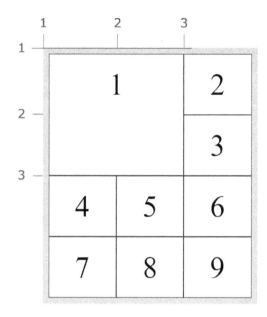

Figure 149: Reserving a larger space for an element within the grid.

This layout was achieved by setting following properties:

```
grid-column-start:1;
grid-column-end:3;
grid-row-start:1;
grid-row-end:3;
```

CSS grid naturally adapts to any screen resolution, but also provides enough properties that can be used to tweak it. In a sense, CSS grid builds on and behaves very similar to `<table>` HTML element but its far more versatile.

13 Chapter XIII: Building HTML Layouts

This chapter will demonstrate creating entire HTML layouts using two of the most popular websites at the writing of this book – *YouTube* and *Twitter*.

I'm not saying that we will create an exact replica of each website with all of the features in their glory. That would take months to do for an experienced team of software engineers and web developers! In fact the server-side and much of the dynamic front-end usually created with JavaScript will be avoided completely. For that, I recommend getting a solid JavaScript book.

Instead, the thinking that goes into *the process* of creating HTML structure and the accompanying CSS styles will be demonstrated here. We will take everything we have learned so far in this book to create these layouts. So if you feel like something doesn't make sense, you can refer to some of the previous chapters of this book.

Let's get started with our first example...

13.1 YouTube Example

The YouTube scaffolding roughly consists of the following structure:

Figure 150: A rough draft of YouTube video page.

The first thing you want to do is to chart out the wireframe of the page. This rough draft will represent the break down of most important components of the layout. It is the guideline you will follow in constructing the page by writing actual HTML code.

13.1.1 Layout Scaffold

The wireframe is rather complex when shown as a whole. Let's break it down into core compartments:

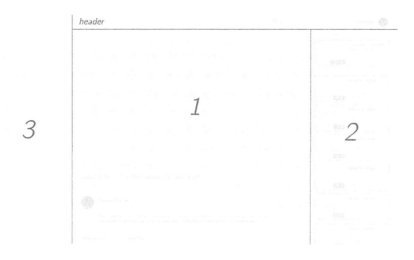

Figure 151: YouTube video page dissected into primary design elements.

Here in *Section 1* we have the main video area. This is also where you will see the channel description box, and just below it users will leave comments.

To the right we see *Section 2* where we have the video suggestions list.

Finally *Section 3* to the left is the overlay pane that appears when the hamburger button right next to the search bar is clicked.

13.1.2 Second Level Elements

We've determined and compartmentalized the parent scaffold – the primary blocks of the entire layout. Now, let's drill down into them and figure out the basic idea behind child elements within each.

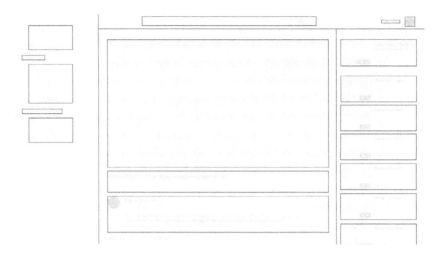

Figure 152: Second level elements in a YouTube-like layout.

Each one of these elements will narrow down on even smaller elements of each User Interface block.

13.1.3 YouTube – Layout Elements

Before going into the source code, let's further dissect the site into these blocks so they can be through of separately:

Figure 153: *YouTube header* or `<div id = "header">`... in the source code.

162

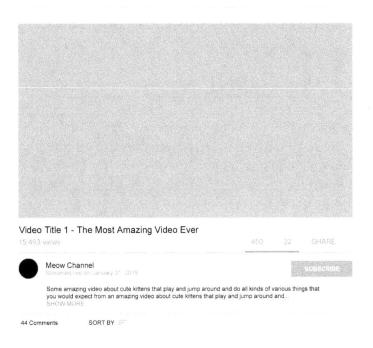

Video Title 1 - The Most Amazing Video Ever

15,493 views   450   22   SHARE

Meow Channel
Streamed live on January 31, 2018

SUBSCRIBE

Some amazing video about cute kittens that play and jump around and do all kinds of various things that
you would expect from an amazing video about cute kittens that play and jump around and...
SHOW MORE

44 Comments   SORT BY

Figure 154: *YouTube primary video area* or `<div id = "primary">...` in the source code. And its children `<div id = "video">...` and `<div id = "video-description">...`

163

Figure 156: An individual video preview block `<div class = "preview">`...
As you can see, in itself this element contains several unique items: the videos'
length, video title, channel name, number of views, and a small label indicating
whether it's a new video – in other words, it has been recently published.

Figure 155: The section containing video suggestions is `<div id =
"secondary">`... and it also contains within itself elements `<div id =
"extras">`..., `<div id = "preview">`..., and a series of `<div class =
"preview">`... elements.

I think we've broken down the layout enough. Now let's write some HTML
code to put it all together!

13.1.4   YouTube – Source Code

This source code listing contains both the CSS and the HTML scaffold work to recreate examples from this chapter.

First, lets open the HTML document with roughly the minimum required code:

```
<html>
  <head>
    <title>YouTube Layout</title>
    <script type = "text/javascript"></script>
  </head>
  <body>

    <style type = "text/css">
```

We've just opened our first style tag. Normally, you would use external CSS file, but for this example we'd like to keep everything in one file for clarity's sake.

```
/* -- Default font for all components -- */
* { font-family: Arial; font-size: 13px; }

/* -- Website's skeleton -- */
#container { position: relative; width: 1200px; margin: auto
    ; }
#body { position: relative;
           width: 1200px;
          margin: auto;
         display: flex;
         padding: 16px;
       box-sizing: border-box; }
#primary { flex-grow: 50; }
#secondary { flex-grow: 1; }
#overlay { position: absolute; }

/* -- Header -- */
#header { display: flex; padding-bottom: 4px; border-bottom:
    1px solid silver; }
```

```css
#header * { flex-grow: 1; }

/* -- YouTube logo -- */
.youtube-logo { display: inline-block; cursor: pointer;   }

/* -- Header elements -- */
#icon-more-container { position: relative; height: 32px; }
.icon-more {
    position: relative;
    display: inline-block;
    width: 28px;
    height: 28px;
    background: url("hamburger.png") no-repeat;
    margin: 3px;
    cursor: pointer;
}
#search-container { position: relative; height: 32px; }
#search-box {
    position: relative;
    margin: 0 auto;
    width: 500px;
    height: 28px;
    border: 1px solid #999;
    border-radius: 3px;
}
#search-input {
    width: 84%;
    height: 28px;
    padding-left: 8px;
    border: 0;
}
#search-button {
    position: relative;
    width: 80px;
    height: 28px;
    float: right;
    background: #D1D1D1 url("magnifying-glass.png") 50% 3px
        no-repeat;
```

```css
}
#username {
    position: relative;
    height: 32px;
    line-height: 32px;
    text-align: right;
}
#small-avatar-container { position: relative; }
.small-avatar { display: relative;
    float: right;
    width: 32px;
    height: 32px;
    background-color: gray;
    border-radius: 32px;
}

/* -- Verical separator line -- */
.separator {
    width: 100%;
    height: 1px;
    border-bottom: 1px solid silver;
    margin-bottom: 10px;
    clear: both;
}

/* -- Video preview box -- */
.preview {
    position: relative;
    width: 275px;
    height: 70px;
    border: 1px solid silver;
    float: right;
    clear: both;
    margin-bottom: 10px;
}
.video-info { padding: 5px; }
.video-box {
    position: relative;
```

```css
        float: left;
        width: 100px;
        height: inherit;
        background: gray;
        margin-right: 5px;
}
.video-length {
        position: absolute;
        bottom: 5px;
        right: 5px;
        width: auto;
        color: white;
        font-size: 12px;
        background: black;
        padding: 1px 3px 1px 3px
}
.preview-video-title { font-weight: bold; }
.secondary-info { font-size: 12px; color: gray; }
.video-info { padding: 5px; }

/* -- Extras -- */
#extras { padding: 5px; height: 20px; }
#up-next { width: 50%; float: left; }
#autoplay { width: 50%; float: right; text-align: right; }

/* -- Video box -- */
#video { width: 850px; height: 500px; background-color:
    silver; }
#video-description { box-sizing: border-box; padding: 32px;
    }
#video-sharebar {
        height: 32px;
        border-bottom: 1px solid gray;
        width: 850px;
}
#video-views { color: gray; }
#share-button {
        width: 80px;
```

```
      float: right;
      text-align: center;
}
#dislikes {
      width: 80px;
      float: right;
      text-align: center;
}
#likes {
      width: 80px;
      float: right;
      border-bottom: 2px solid gray;
      text-align: center;
}

/* -- Disable text selection in video preview card -- */
#secondary * {
-webkit-touch-callout: none; /* iOS Safari */
-webkit-user-select: none; /* Safari */
-khtml-user-select: none; /* Konqueror HTML */
-moz-user-select: none; /* Firefox */
-ms-user-select: none; /* Internet Explorer/Edge */
user-select: none; /* Non-prefixed version, currently
supported by Chrome and Opera */
}

/* -- Comment -- */
.comment { display: flex; padding-top: 16px; }
.comment-avatar { flex-grow: 1; margin-right: 16px; }
.comment-username { font-weight: bold; }
.comment-body-container { flex-grow: 50; }
.comment-body { padding-top: 8px; }
.comment-replies { font-weight: bold; margin-top: 8px;
    cursor: pointer; }

/* -- Autoplay switcher -- */
#autoplay-switch-container {
      position: relative;
```

```css
    display: inline-block;
    width: 50px;
    height: 16px;
    border: 1px solid gray;
    border-radius: 16px;
    background: gray;
    cursor: pointer;
}
#autoplay-switch {
    position: absolute;
    top: 0;
    left: 0;
    width: 14px;
    height: 14px;
    border-radius: 32px;
    border: 1px solid gray;
    background: white;
}
#autoplay-switch.on {
    left: unset;
    right: 0 !important;
}

#channel-info-container { position: relative; padding: 10px;
    }
#channel-info { margin-left: 50px; }

#video-about { clear: both; padding: 16px 0 16px 0; }
#video-avatar {
    position: relative;
    float: left;
    display: block;
    width: 32px;
    height: 32px;
    background-color: gray;
    border-radius: 32px;
}
#subscribe-button {
```

```css
    float: right;
    position: relative;
    display: block;
    background: gray;
    color: white;
    text-align: center;
    font-family: Arial, sans-serif;
    padding: 1px 10px 1px 10px;
    line-height: 32px;
    cursor: pointer;
}

/* -- Overlay -- */
#overlay-container {
    display: none;
    position: fixed;
    top: 0;
    left: 0;
    width: 100%;
    height: 100%;
    background-color: rgba(0, 0, 0, 0.5);
}
#overlay-container.on {
    display: block !important;
}
#overlay {
    background-color: white;
    padding: 32px;
    height: 100%;
}
```

HTML source code listing follows:

```html
  </style>

<!-- Main view //-->

<div id = "container">
  <div id = "header">
```

```
<div id = "icon−more−container"
onclick = "document.getElementById('overlay−container').
    className␣=␣'on';">
  <div class = "icon−more"></div>
</div>
<img class = "youtube−logo"
...src = "youtube−logo.png"
...alt = "YouTube␣Logo" />
<div id = "search−container"
..style = "flex−grow:␣7;">
  <div id = "search−box">
    <input type = "text"
        .id = "search−input"
    placeholder = "Search␣YouTube"/>
    <div id = "search−button"></div>
  </div>
</div>
<div id = "username" style = "flex−grow:␣2;">username</div
  >
<div id = "small−avatar−container">
  <div class = "small−avatar"></div>
</div>
</div>

<div id = "body">
  <div id = "primary">
    <div id = "video"></div>
    <div>
    <h1>Video Part 1 − The Most Amazing Video Ever</h1>
    </div>
    <div id = "video−sharebar">
      <div id = "video−views">15,493 views</div>
      <div id = "share−button">SHARE</div>
      <div id = "dislikes">22</div>
      <div id = "likes">450</div>
    </div>
    <div id = "video−description">
      <div id = "channel−info−container">
```

```
    <div id = "subscribe−button">SUBSCRIBE</div>
    <div id = "video−avatar"></div>
    <div id = "channel−info">Meow Channel<br/>Streamed
        live on January 31, 2018</div>
</div>

<div id = "video−about">Some amazing video footage
    about cute kittens that play and jump around and do
     all kinds of various things that you would expect
    from an amazing video about cute kittens that play
    and jump around and...</div>

<div class = "separator"></div>
44 Comments <span style = "width:␣50px;␣display:␣
    inline−block;"></span>
SORT BY <img src = "stats.png" alt = "stats" />
<!−− comment 1 //−−>
<div class = "comment">
  <div class = "comment−avatar">
    <div class = "small−avatar"></div>
  </div>
  <div class = "comment−body−container">
    <span class = "comment−username">London Grammar</
        span>
    <span class = "comment−timestamp">4 years ago</
        span>
    <div class = "comment−body">And when your house
        begins to rust<br/>Oh, it's just, metal and
        dust.</div>
    <div class = "comment−replies">View all 4 replies<
        /div>
  </div>
</div>

<!−− comment 2 //−−>
<div class = "comment">
  <div class = "comment−avatar">
    <div class = "small−avatar"></div>
```

```
      </div>
      <div class = "comment-body-container">
        <span class = "comment-username">Someone Else</
           span>
        <span class = "comment-timestamp">4 years ago</
           span>
        <div class = "comment-body">This is just another
           comment.</div>
        <div class = "comment-replies">View 1 reply</div>
      </div>
    </div>


    <!-- comment 3 //-->
    <div class = "comment">
      <div class = "comment-avatar">
        <div class = "small-avatar"></div>
      </div>
      <div class = "comment-body-container">
        <span class = "comment-username">
          Furry Visitor
        </span> <span class = "comment-timestamp">4 years
           ago</span>
        <div class = "comment-body">More opinions about
           this amazing video.</div>
        <div class = "comment-replies">View all 3 replies<
           /div>
      </div>
    </div>
  </div>
</div>

<div id = "secondary">
  <div id = "extras">
    <div id = "up-next">Up next</div>
    <div id = "autoplay">
      <div id = "autoplay-switch-container">
        <div id = "autoplay-switch"
        onclick = "this.className == 'on' ?
```

```
                              this.className = '' :
                              this.className = 'on'"></div>
        </div>
      </div>
    </div>

    <div class = "preview">
      <div class = "video-box">
        <div class = "video-length">01:51:28</div>
      </div>
      <div class = "video-info">
        <span class = "preview-video-title">
          Video Title 1 - The Most Amazing Video Ever
        </span><br/>
        <span class = "secondary-info">
          Meow Channel
        </span><br/>
        <span class = "secondary-info">1.1K views</span>
      </div>
    </div>

    <div class = "separator"></div>

    <div class = "preview">
      <div class = "video-box">
        <div class = "video-length">01:51:28</div>
      </div>
      <div class = "video-info">
        <span class = "preview-video-title">
          Video Part 2 - The Most Amazing Video Ever
        </span><br/>
        <span class = "secondary-info">Meow Channel</span>
        <br/>
        <span class = "secondary-info">1.1K views</span>
      </div>
    </div>

    <!-- Repeat the block above 7 times to create a list
```

```
                -- web developers usually use "iterators" connected
                to a database in order to scroll through an
                existing list of videos (or other items.) //-->

        </div>
      </div>
    </div>

    <!-- Overlay //-->
    <div id = "overlay-container" class = "">
      <div id = "overlay">
        <div class = "icon-more" onclick = "document.
            getElementById('overlay-container').className = '';">
          </div>
        <img class = "youtube-logo" src = "youtube-logo.png" alt
            = "YouTube Logo" />
        <ul>
          <li>Home</li>
          <li>Trending</li>
          <li>Subscription</li>
        </ul>
        LIBRARY
        <ul>
          <li>History</li>
          <li>Watch later</li>
          <li>WebGL Tutorials</li>
          <li>React JS Tutorials</li>
          <li>Show more</li>
        </ul>
        SUBSCRIPTIONS
        <ul>
          <li>Cats Incorporated</li>
          <li>Meowing Recordings</li>
          <li>The Meow Channel</li>
        </ul>
      </div>
    </div>
```

</body>
</html>

It took us about 4 pages of code to construct a basic YouTube layout.

Running this code in a browser will produce the following result:

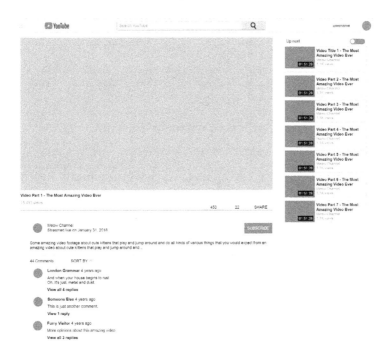

Figure 157: Actual HTML and CSS rendered in Chrome browser. Note the autoplay switch actually works here! Thanks to the CSS and some inline *JavaScript* code.

13.2 Twitter Example

In this chapter we will create another layout. This time we will be learning from Twitter – one of the most popular social network sites – as of this writing. If you haven't used Twitter before, there is a good chance you have at least heard of it.

Figure 158: Twitter-like layout.

Following the same principle of separating design element by breaking them down into individual sections – we can think of Twitter layout as consisting of these core elements:

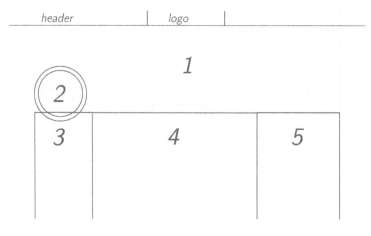

Figure 159: Twitter layout broken down into sections.

13.2.1 Twitter – Breaking down the layout into sections

Figure 160: Header is an essential component of any modern web application or website. Twitter is no exception from this rule. In source code that we're about to see this location will be created with `<div id = "navigation-container">...` and `<div id = "navigation">...` HTML elements.

Figure 161: Main profile header area.

Figure 162: Avatar.

Meowing Meowzer

@meowzer

Sittin' here all day, waiting for
you to pick me up. I am the
meowing meowzer looking for a
new home. Please take me.

☐ Joined January 2018
☐ 7 Photos and videos

Figure 163: An area under the avatar with user profile details and photo gallery.

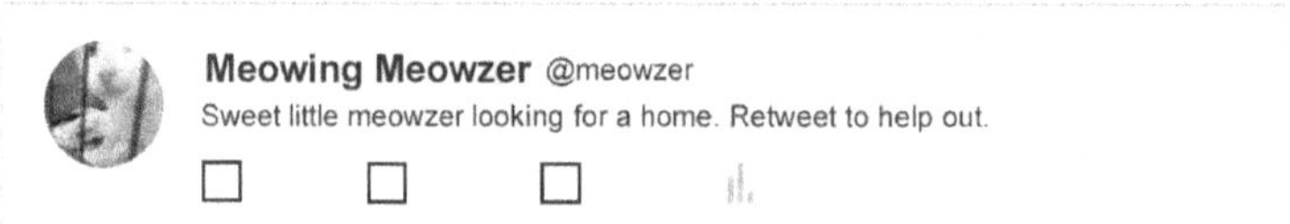

Meowing Meowzer @meowzer
Sweet little meowzer looking for a home. Retweet to help out.
☐   ☐   ☐

Figure 164: An individual tweet.

Tweets	Following	Followers	Likes	Lists	Moments
2,135	1,399	955	2,299	3	1

Edit profile

Figure 165: Secondary navigation bar.

Lets build out these elements with HTML and CSS. The complete source code is listed in the next section.

13.2.2 Twitter – Source code

The source code for Twitter website is a bit more simple than YouTube.

```html
<html>
<head>
<title>YouTube Layout</title>
<script type = "text/javascript"></script>
</head>
<body>

<style type = "text/css">

  body { margin: 0; padding: 0; }
  body * {   }

  /* -- Default font for all components -- */
  * { font-family: Arial; font-size: 13px; }

  /* -- Website's skeleton -- */
  #container {
    display: grid;
    position: relative;
    width: 1200px;
    height: auto;
    margin: auto;
    border: 2px solid blue;
  }

  #navigation-container {
    position: fixed;
    top: 0;
    left: 0;
    height: 40px;
    width: 100%;
    border: 2px solid blue;
    background: white;
    z-index: 1;
  }
```

```css
#navigation {
    position: relative;
    width: 1200px;
    margin: auto;
    border: 2px solid red;
}

#navigation div {
    display: inline-block;
    padding: 10px;
}

.sub-navigation-container-1 {
    margin-left: 298px;
    margin-bottom: 16px;
    height: 37px;
    border: 1px solid gray;
    background: white;
}

.sub-navigation-container-1 div {
    display: inline-block;
    padding: 10px;
}

.sub-navigation-container-2 {
    margin-left: 0px;
    margin-bottom: 16px;
    height: 37px;
    border: 1px solid gray;
    background: white;
}

.sub-navigation-container-2 div {
    display: inline-block;
    padding: 10px;
}
```

```css
#header {
  background: url('profile-image.jpg');
  height: 375px;
}

#body {
  position: relative;
  width: 1200px;
  margin: auto;
  padding: 8px;
  box-sizing: border-box;
  display: grid;
  grid-gap: 10px;
  grid-template-columns: 280px auto 250px;
}

#overlay-container { position: fixed; }
#overlay { position: absolute; }

/*-- tweet -- */
.tweet {
  position: relative;
  display: grid;
  padding-left: 30px;
  grid-template-columns: 50px auto;
  margin-bottom: 16px;
}

.tweet-avatar {
  position: relative;
  width: 48px;
  height: 48px;
  background: gray;
  border-radius: 100px;
}

.tweet-message {
```

```css
  display: inline-block;
  width: 400px;
  min-height: 50px;
  margin-left: 8px;
}

.tweet-username {
  display: block;
  margin-bottom: 4px;
  font-weight: bold;
  min-height: 18px;
}

.tweet-options { margin-top: 16px; }

.option {
  width: 16px;
  height: 16px;
  border: 2px solid silver;
  display: inline-block;
  margin: 0 16px
}

#avatar-circle-1 {
  position: absolute;
  top: -200px;
  left: 64px;
  width: 200px;
  height: 200px;
  background: white;
  border-radius: 150px;
  border: 2px solid silver;
}

#avatar-circle-2 {
  position: absolute;
  top: 13px;
  left: 13px;
```

```css
    width: 170px;
    height: 170px;
    background: url("meow.png");
    background-size: 100% 100%;
    border-radius: 150px;
    border: 2px solid silver;
  }

  .selected-tab { border-bottom: 2px solid gray; }

  .sub-container {
    border: 1px solid gray;
    border-radius: 3px;
    padding: 5px;
  }
</style>

<!-- fixed header //-->
<div id = "navigation-container">
  <div id = "navigation">
    <div>Home</div>
    <div>Moments</div>
    <div>Navigation</div>
    <div>Messages</div>
    <div>Logo</div>
    <div>Search</div>
    <div>Avatar</div>
    <div>Tweet</div>
  </div>
</div>

<!-- Main view //-->
<div id = "container">
  <div id = "header">header</div>
  <div class = "sub-navigation-container-1">
  <div>button 1</div>
  <div>button 2</div>
  <div class = "selected-tab">button 3</div>
```

```html
<div>button 4</div>
<div>button 5</div>
<div>button 6</div>
</div>
<div id = "body">

<!-- profile details //-->
<div id = "profile-details">

<div id = "avatar-circle-1">
<div id = "avatar-circle-2"></div>
</div>

<div class = "sub-container">
Meowing Meowzer<br/>
@meowmeowzer
</div>

<div class = "sub-container">
Sitting there waiting for someone to pick me up. I am the
    meowing meowzer, please take me home.
</div>

</div>

<!-- message feed //-->
<div id = "feed">

  <div class = "sub-navigation-container-2">
    <div class = "selected-tab">Tweets</div>
    <div>Tweets & replies</div>
    <div>Media</div>
  </div>

  <div class = "tweet">
    <div class = "tweet-avatar"></div>
    <div class = "tweet-message">
    <div class = "tweet-username">Meowing Meowzer</div>
```

```html
<div class = "tweet-body">This is quite a message and
    O what a message this is.<br/>Maybe this is second
    line.</div>
<div class = "tweet-options">
<div class = "option"></div>
<div class = "option"></div>
<div class = "option"></div>
</div>
</div>
</div>

<div class = "tweet">
  <div class = "tweet-avatar"></div>
  <div class = "tweet-message">
    <div class = "tweet-username">Meowing Meowzer</div>
    <div class = "tweet-body">This is quite a message
        and O what a message this is.<br/>Maybe this is
        second line.</div>
    <div class = "tweet-options">
      <div class = "option"></div>
      <div class = "option"></div>
      <div class = "option"></div>
    </div>
  </div>
</div>

<div class = "tweet">
  <div class = "tweet-avatar"></div>
  <div class = "tweet-message">
    <div class = "tweet-username">Meowing Meowzer</div>
    <div class = "tweet-body">This is quite a message
        and O what a message this is.<br/>Maybe this is
        second line.</div>
    <div class = "tweet-options">
      <div class = "option"></div>
      <div class = "option"></div>
      <div class = "option"></div>
    </div>
```

```
        </div>
      </div>

    </div>

    <!-- sidebar //-->
    <div id = "sidebar">sidebar</div>
    </div>
  </div>
</body>
</html>
```

These examples only demonstrate construction of HTML layouts. Building entire applications requires additional knowledge of *JavaScript* and server-side programming.

This code was included here at the last chapters of this book, to give the reader an idea of what's involved in creating realistic website layouts.

In the next section, we will explore creation of a couple simple web applications: *Clock* and *Calculator*, respectively. The goal of the author here is to show potential next steps that the reader new to HTML should explore, if he (*or she of course*) is interested in skill-set expansion required for creating web applications professionally.

14   Chapter XIV: Building Web Applications

Even though this book is only an introduction to HTML language it wouldn't be fair to the reader if we didn't show any examples of small applications at all.

While we won't be building full blown applications here, the examples provided here will serve as a starting point to crafting something more interesting than basic layouts.

The purpose of this chapter was intended to demonstrate the place of HTML in overall application composition consisting of two other languages: CSS and JavaScript.

14.1 Clock

By the end of this section we will create this simple clock:

Figure 166: The notches and clock hands are actually HTML elements positioned using combination of techniques covered in this book.

No images were used in creation of this clock. Everything is a `DIV` element. Here is the same clock with `border: 1px solid black;` and `background: white;` properties that expose its wireframe structure:

Figure 167: Wireframe view of the HTML clock showing transparent elements.

Head over to this jsFiddle URL created to see how this clock works in action:
https://jsfiddle.net/7ngueqh8/134/

To create this clock application, we need to separate our code in three distinct parts: HTML for *semantic structure*, CSS for determining *position, rotation angles and size* of elements, and JavaScript for *animating the clock hands*.

14.1.1 HTML – Semantic Structure

HTML is the simplest part of the application:

```
 1  <div id = "clock-rim">
 2    <div id = "clock-base">
 3      <div id = "notch-container"></div>
 4      <div id = "brand">HTML<br/>clock</div>
 5      <div id = "hour"></div>
 6      <div id = "minute"></div>
 7      <div id = "second"></div>
 8      <div id = "center"></div>
 9    </div>
10  </div>
```

14.1.2 CSS – Element Style

```
 1  /* — Outer area of the clock — */
 2  #clock-rim {
 3    display: block;
 4    position: relative;
 5    width: 300px;
 6    height: 300px;
 7    background: linear-gradient(gray, black);
 8    border-radius: 150px;
 9  }
10
11  /* — Inner area of the clock — */
12  #clock-base {
13    display: block;
```

```
14    position: relative;
15    width: 260px;
16    height: 260px;
17    margin: 19px auto;
18    border−radius: 150px;
19    background: white;
20  }
21
22  /* −− Seconds hand −− */
23  #second { position: absolute; top: 123px; left: 128px; width
       : 100px; height: 2px; border: 1px solid transparent;
       border−radius: 5px; transform: unset; background: green;
       transform−origin: 1px 1px; }
24
25  /* −− Minutes hand −− */
26  #minute { position: absolute; top: 123px; left: 128px; width
       : 100px; height: 4px; border: 1px solid transparent;
       border−radius: 5px; transform: unset; background: red;
       transform−origin: 2px 2px; }
27
28  /* −− Hours hand −− */
29  #hour { position: absolute; top: 123px; left: 128px; width:
       50px; height: 4px; border: 1px solid transparent; border−
       radius: 5px; transform: unset; background: blue;
       transform−origin: 2px 2px; }
30
31  /* −− Center of the clock −− */
32  #center { position: absolute; top: 118px; left: 120px; width
       : 16px; height: 16px; background: white; border: 1px
       solid gray; border−radius: 16px; }
33
34  /* −− The box that says "HTML clock" −− */
35  #brand { position: absolute; top: 110px; left: 165px; border
       : 1px solid gray; border−radius: 5px; width: 50px; height
       : 40px; font−family: Verdana; font−size: 11px; text−align
       : center; line−height: 20px; }
36
37  #notch−container {
```

```
38    width:  260px;
39    height:  260px
40  }
41
42  /* -- Thick notch (hours and minutes) -- */
43  .notch {
44    position: absolute;
45    width:  10px;
46    height:  2px;
47    background:  black;
48    border-radius:  5px 5px 5px 5px;
49  }
50
51  /* -- Thin notch (seconds) -- */
52  .thin {
53    position: absolute;
54    width:  10px;
55    height:  1px;
56    border-top:  1px solid gray;
57  }
58
59  div { border:  1px solid transparent; }
```

14.1.3   JavaScript – Animating CSS Styles

Finally, this JavaScript will animate the clock's hands.

The notable code here is the `setInterval` JavaScript function that runs the code specified inside so-called "arrow function" brackets ()=>{...}. A couple of functions for converting vectors to angles and back are provided. These are useful whenever you need to add custom-rotated elements to your design.

One other thing of interest you may find here:

```
1     var notch = document.createElement("div");
```

Notice how the JavaScript method document.createElement("div"); dynamically creates an HTML element to be implanted into the DOM (using `element.appendChild(notch)` function) alongside other existing elements.

193

In JavaScript, you can create HTML elements dynamically, without having to write HTML code. This is a slightly advanced subject and it will require additional material beyond the scope of this book.

Unfortunately I cannot go any deeper in detail here and I hope you can pick up a good JavaScript book if you're interested in further exploring the subject of building interactive web applications.

```
1  /* — This function converts degrees to radians — */
2  function deg2rad(d)
3  {
4    return (2 * d / 360) * Math.PI;
5  }
6
7  let H = 0;
8  let M = 0;
9  let S = 0;
10
11 /* — Start updating the clock at an interval — */
12 setInterval(()=>{
13
14   let minute = document.getElementById("minute");
15   let hour = document.getElementById("hour");
16   let second = document.getElementById("second");
17
18   S = new Date().getSeconds() * 6 - 90;
19   M = new Date().getMinutes() * 6 - 90;
20   H = new Date().getHours() * 30 - 90;
21
22   second.style.transform = 'rotate(' + S + 'deg)';
23   minute.style.transform = 'rotate(' + M + 'deg)';
24   hour.style.transform = 'rotate(' + H + 'deg)';
25
26 }, 10);
27
28 /* — Convert 2D vector to angle — */
29 function vec2ang(x, y) {
30   angleInRadians = Math.atan2(y, x);
31   angleInDegrees = (angleInRadians / Math.PI) * 180.0;
```

```
32    return angleInDegrees ;
33  }
34
35  /* --- Convert  angle  to  2D  vector --- */
36  function  ang2vec ( angle )  {
37    var  radians  =  angle  *  (Math. PI  /  180.0) ;
38    var  x  =  Math. cos ( radians ) ;
39    var  y  =  Math. sin ( radians ) ;
40    var  a  =  new  Segment (0 ,  0 ,  x ,  y ) ;
41    var  u  =  a. normal () . unit () ;
42    return  [u. vecx ,  u. vecy ] ;
43  }
44
45  let  nc  =  document. getElementById ("notch−container") ;
46  let  angle  =  0;
47  let  rotate_x  =  120;
48  let  rotate_y  =  0;
49
50  /* --- Arrange  thin  second  notches  around  the  clock's  face ---
         */
51  for  (let  i  =  0;  i  <  60;  i++)  {
52    let  thin  =  document. createElement ("div") ;
53    let  x  =  rotate_x  *  Math. cos ( angle )  −  rotate_y  *  Math. cos (
           angle )
54    let  y  =  rotate_y  *  Math. cos ( angle )  +  rotate_x  *  Math. sin (
           angle )
55    let  r  =  vec2ang (x ,  y ) ;
56    thin. className  =  "thin" ;
57    thin.style. left  =  122  +  x  +  "px" ;
58    thin.style. top  =  127  +  y  +  "px" ;
59    thin.style. transform  =  "rotate (" +  r  +  "deg)" ;
60    nc. appendChild ( thin ) ;
61    angle  +=   (Math. PI  /  300)  *  10;
62  }
63
64  // reset
65  angle  =  0;
66  rotate_x  =  120;
```

```
67   rotate_y = 0;
68
69   /* —— Arrange thicker notches around the clock's face —— */
70   for (let i = 0; i < 12; i++) {
71     let notch = document.createElement("div");
72     let x = rotate_x * Math.cos(angle) − rotate_y * Math.cos(
          angle)
73     let y = rotate_y * Math.cos(angle) + rotate_x * Math.sin(
          angle)
74     let r = vec2ang(x, y);
75     notch.className = "notch";
76     notch.style.left = 122 + x + "px";
77     notch.style.top = 127 + y + "px";
78     notch.style.transform = "rotate(" + r + "deg)";
79     nc.appendChild(notch);
80     angle += (Math.PI / 60) * 10;
81   }
```

We already discussed in the beginning of this book in section *2.19 Including Inline, Internal and External CSS or JavaScript Code* the placement of CSS and JavaScript blocks in your HTML page. Head over there to see where exactly each part of this web application should be entered in your source code.

14.2 Calculator

In our previous example we created an animated clock. But it's not really an *interactive* application. Meaning, it does not offer the visitor a chance to interact with it or take some sort of input.

In this chapter, let's create another simple application that takes basic input from the user. This calculator application should be interesting-enough to demonstrate user input without having to deal with too much complexity.

First, let's take a look at what we're actually trying to build here:

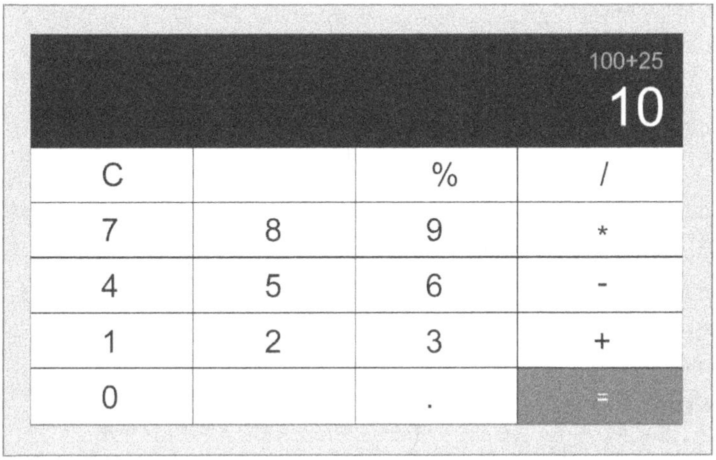

Figure 168: Calculator application we will build in this section of the book.

Let's begin by building out the HTML scaffold!

14.2.1 HTML – Application Scaffold

The HTML here is the simplest part of the entire application. We just need to add the view and some buttons. Note that no id's are necessary for most of the buttons. This is because our JavaScript code will read the values directly from the element's content from the `event.target` object via the `onClick` event.

197

```
 1  <div id = "frame">
 2    <div id = "calculator">
 3      <div id = "history">0</div>
 4      <div id = "view">0</div>
 5      <div id = "buttons">
 6        <div id = "reset">C</div>
 7        <div></div>
 8        <div></div>
 9        <div>/</div>
10        <div>7</div>
11        <div>8</div>
12        <div>9</div>
13        <div>*</div>
14        <div>4</div>
15        <div>5</div>
16        <div>6</div>
17        <div>-</div>
18        <div>1</div>
19        <div>2</div>
20        <div>3</div>
21        <div>+</div>
22        <div></div>
23        <div>0</div>
24        <div>.</div>
25        <div id = "equals">=</div>
26      </div>
27    </div>
28    <div id = "on"></div>
29  </div>
30  <div id = "message"></div>
31  <div id = "message2"></div>
```

14.2.2   CSS – Cascading Style Sheets

```
1  * { font-family: Arial, sans-serif; }
2
3  #frame {
```

```
 4      position: relative;
 5      display: block;
 6      width: 500px;
 7      height: 244px;
 8      padding: 16px;
 9      background: gray;
10      border-radius: 8px;
11      background: linear-gradient(#555, #000);
12  }
13
14  #calculator {
15      position: relative;
16      display: block;
17      width: 500px;
18      height: 400px;
19      margin-top: 29px;
20  }
21
22  #history {
23      width: 100%;
24      height: 16px;
25      background: #333;
26      color: #999;
27      text-align: right;
28  }
29
30  #view {
31      width: 100%;
32      height: 28px;
33      background: #333;
34      color: #CCC;
35      text-align: right;
36      font-size: 20px;
37  }
38
39  #buttons {
40      display: grid;
41      grid-template-columns: auto auto auto auto
```

```
42  }
43
44  #buttons * {
45      cursor: pointer;
46      background: white;
47      text-align: center;
48      height: 32px;
49      line-height: 32px;
50  }
51
52  #buttons * {
53      border: 1px solid #aaa;
54      border-right: unset;
55      border-bottom: unset;
56  }
57
58  #buttons *:hover {
59      background: lime;
60      color: #333;
61      font-weight: bold;
62  }
63
64  #buttons * {
65      -webkit-touch-callout: none; /* iOS Safari */
66      -webkit-user-select: none; /* Safari */
67      -khtml-user-select: none; /* Konqueror HTML */
68      -moz-user-select: none; /* Firefox */
69      -ms-user-select: none; /* Internet Explorer/Edge */
70      user-select: none; /* Non-prefixed version, currently
71      supported by Chrome and Opera */
72  }
73
74  #buttons * {
75      background: linear-gradient(#fff, #bbb);
76  }
77
78  #reset {
79      background: yellow;
```

```
80  }
81
82  #equals {
83      background: blue;
84      color: white;
85  }
86
87  #on {
88      position: absolute;
89      top: 8px;
90      right: 8px;
91      width: 8px;
92      height: 8px;
93      background: linear-gradient(lime, green);
94      border-radius: 16px;
95      border: 1px solid #000;
96  }
```

14.2.3 JavaScript – Programming Interactivity

Below is the JavaScript listing that turns the HTML and CSS we constructed so far into a fully functioning calculator!

```
1
2   var queue = new Array();
3   var current_number = new Array();
4   var gid = document.getElementById;
5   var tally = 0;
6
7   function print_queue() {
8       document.getElementById("message").innerHTML = JSON.
            stringify(queue); }
9
10  function print_current() {
11      document.getElementById("message2").innerHTML =
            array_to_number(current_number); }
12
13  function array_to_number(number) {
14      return number.toString().replace(/,/gi, ""); }
```

```
15
16   function reset_history () {
17     document.getElementById("history").innerHTML = ""; }
18
19   function update_history () {
20     document.getElementById("history").innerHTML = queue.
           toString().replace(/,/gi, ""); }
21
22   let can_use_actions = false;
23   let can_use_digits = true;
24
25   Object.entries(document.querySelectorAll("#buttons_div")).
         map((element) => {
26
27     element[1].addEventListener("click", function(event) {
28
29     let value = event.target.innerHTML;
30
31     if (value == "." && current_number.indexOf(".") == -1)
32       current_number.push(".");
33
34     // Digit was pressed -- but don't process it if digits
           cannot be used at this time
35     if (can_use_digits) {
36       if (!isNaN(value) && value != "") {
37       current_number.push(value);
38       document.getElementById("view").innerHTML =
             array_to_number(current_number);
39       print_queue();
40       print_current();
41       // At least one digit was entered, we can use actions
             again
42       can_use_actions = true;
43       }
44     }
45
46     switch (event.target.innerHTML)
47     {
```

```
48       case 'C':
49         // Reset view
50         document.getElementById("view").innerHTML = "0";
51         queue = new Array();
52         current_number = new Array();
53         can_use_actions = false;
54         can_use_digits = true;
55       break;
56
57       case '=':
58
59         // Reset view
60         var -complete = (queue.toString() + current_number).
               replace(/,/gi, "");
61         queue = new Array();
62         current_number = new Array();
63
64         // Assign result to current number in queue
65         var evaluated = eval(complete);
66         document.getElementById("view").innerHTML = evaluated;
67         current_number[0] = evaluated;
68         reset_history();
69
70         // We just calculated result,
71         // This result becomes the first number in the queue
72         // Disable digits... and enable actions (+-/*)
73         can_use_actions = true;
74         can_use_digits = false;
75       break;
76
77       case '*':
78         if (can_use_actions) {
79           queue.push(array_to_number(current_number));
80           current_number = new Array();
81           queue.push("*");
82           can_use_actions = false;
83           can_use_digits = true;
84         }
```

```
85        break;
86
87     case '/':
88        if (can_use_actions) {
89           queue.push(array_to_number(current_number));
90           current_number = new Array();
91           queue.push("/");
92           can_use_actions = false;
93           can_use_digits = true;
94        }
95     break;
96
97     case '+':
98        if (can_use_actions) {
99           queue.push(array_to_number(current_number));
100          current_number = new Array();
101          queue.push("+");
102          can_use_actions = false;
103          can_use_digits = true;
104       }
105    break;
106
107    case '-':
108       if (can_use_actions) {
109          queue.push(array_to_number(current_number));
110          current_number = new Array();
111          queue.push("-");
112          can_use_actions = false;
113          can_use_digits = true;
114       }
115    break;
116
117    default:
118       update_history();
119    break;
120    }
121
122    print_queue();
```

```
123
124    });
125
126  });
```

See this app in action at `https://jsfiddle.net/wx695acf/163/`

15 Chapter XV: Creating Meaningful Websites

Semantic structure of your HTML document helps search engines increase the chance of correctly categorizing your website so that it is easily found by people.

Web designers rarely think of semantic structure of their website, focusing primarily on designing layouts visually and populating them with content and media. But in addition, a semantically correct HTML document harbors following advantages:

1. **Friendship with Search Engines.** Even if Google changes their search algorithm, a semantically correct website has better chance of keeping a higher position in search results, compared to a similar website that does not implement a semantic strategy.

2. **Social Media.** Semantically-correct websites provide *helpful hints* that improve experience with your site. For example, you can include special images, additional title and description apart from standard meta tags. This provides ability to use different title and description for the specific case when your page is shared social media websites, such as Facebook or Twitter.

3. **Serving Wider Audience.** Creating better experience for people with disabilities, by – for example – specifying audible text describing visual elements for visitors with compromised vision.

You can improve semantic integrity of your website by using *meta tags*.

15.1 MetaTags

Meta tags provide additional information about your web page. They are used in a wide variety of ways, some of which we'll take a look at below.

All meta tags are *required* to be specified between the `<head></head>` pair in your HTML document.

But your HTML document itself is not required to use any of the meta tags at all. However, it is in your best interest to do so if you want to improve the way in which search engines process and categorize your website.

Including a few meta tags is better than not including any at all. Some meta tags have greater influence on different aspects of website readability by web servers. While others are not significant at all.

Here is a collection of meta tags you will find yourself working with.

```
1  <meta name = "language" content = "English">
```

A meta tag to specify the default language of your web page.

```
1  <meta http-equiv = "content-language" content="en-US" />
```

Specify content language, this time in another format, usually more often used by web servers.

```
1  <meta
2  http-equiv = "Content-Type"
3     content = "text/html;charset=utf-8">
```

Let browser know the text formatting character set assumes UTF-8.

```
1  <meta name = "viewport" content = "width=device-width"/>
```

A directive for mobile phones, to set width of the website to the width of the device.

```
1  <meta name = "description"
2     content = "This_is_a_tutorial_library_site_which_contains
        _a_collection_of_useful_React_tutorials._React_is_a_
        JavaScript_library_for_developing_web_applications_
        efficiently."/>
```

The description meta tag provides a few paragraphs about the content of the web page. Be as descriptive as possible.

```
1  <meta name = "keywords"
2      content = "react , reactjs , js , docs , documentation , intro , ui ,
           native , pdf , book , e−book , tutorial , free , course , future
           ,2017 , project , javascript , welcome , getting , started , book ,
           review" />
```

A series of single keywords describing your website. They can be separated by comma or space character.

Please ensure that each keyword refers to content that actually exists on that web page! It is not a good idea to bloat this meta tag with keywords in an attempt to gain more attention from search engines. Artificial Intelligence algorithms developed at Google are very apt at figuring out whether someone is trying to play the system.

```
1  <meta name = "author"
2      content = "Greg_Sidelnikov" />
```

Author of the content.

```
1  <meta name = "subject"
2      content = "React_JS_Full_Stack_Web_Development" />
```

Subject of this web page.

```
1  <meta name = "copyright"
2      content = "Learning_Curve_Books , _LLC" />
```

Copyright information.

```
1  <meta name = "web_author"
2      content = "Greg_Sidelnikov">
```

Web author.

```
1  <meta name = "robots"
2      content = "index , _follow" />
```

A hint for search engines (spider robot software that "crawls" the web) on how you wish your content to be treated.

The `index` directive means you want Google or other search engines to *index* your website in their search engine. In other words *store* it in their database used for showing search results – which opens doors to driving more traffic and potentially targeted visitors to the content of your site.

The `follow` directive suggests to the spider to also visit all hyperlinks on your website for potential inclusion in web search.

You can specify a value of `noindex, nofollow` if you want to prevent search engines from indexing your web page, or following any hyperlinks. However, you can also set this value to `follow` if you don't want the page to be indexed, but wish for the search engines to follow through to any of the pages specified in hyperlinks on that page.

```
1  <meta name = "abstract"
2      content = "quick,start,guide,beginners,tutorial"/>
```

An abstract idea of your web page specified using a list of keywords separated by comma or space. Similar to `keywords` meta tag.

```
1  <meta name = "revisit-after" content = "3 days"/>
```

A hint for search engines about how often you wish them to re-visit your page. This is often ignored by search engines. It is unknown whether this meta tag is taken seriously by any of the modern search engines, as they are keen on deciding on these types of rules on their own.

```
1  <meta name = "contact"
2      content = "greg.sidelnikov@gmail.com"  />
```

Physical address, P.O. Box or an e-mail address the author of this web page wants its visitors to refer to when contacting them.

```
1  <meta name = "distribution" content = "global"  />
```

Specify global distribution.

```
1  <meta name = "news_keywords"
2      content = "Online, ReactJS, React, JS, Tutorial, Guide,
          Quick, Start, Introduction, Beginners"  />
```

Keywords used in news stories referring to your page. This tag is also not used very much, but with advent of the recent battle on "fake news," web designers might want to take greater care at thinking up of a list of keywords that talks about the web page in the context of a news story.

```
1  <meta name = "rating" content = "general" />
2  <meta name = "rating" content = "safe_for_kids" />
```

A tag used to rate how appropriate the content of your web page is for a specific audience. When used, it is used to let younger audience know that the content may or may not be appropriate for them.

This is not a common meta tag by any degree and carries no practical influence on your website. But it's nice to know that it exists, because as the web matures, features like these might become more important with time.

```
1  <meta name = "verify-v1" content = "123" />
```

The verify-v1 tag is often used by Google and some other service providers, to verify that the website belongs to its owner.

The content value is usually given by the service provider, for you to paste into your site. Because this step requires *logging into your web server* Google or other companies can be sure that you are the web site's owner.

Once that is determined, those companies will allow access to various features regarding the domain name of your site that are otherwise not available. This adds a great deal of security, limiting certain permissions to actual owners of the website.

```
1  <meta name = "google-site-verification" content = "567" />
```

Another way to verify ownership of a website by a Google service, for example, Google Webmasters (http://www.google.com/webmasters)

15.1.1 Facebook Post Preview

```
1  <meta property="og:title" content="React.js_Tutorials"/>
2  <meta property="og:type" content="article"/>
3  <meta property="og:url" content="http://www.example.net/"/>
4  <meta property="og:site_name" content="React_JS_Tutorials"/>
5  <meta property="og:image"
6          content="http://www.example.net/react-logo.png" />
```

A series of meta tags developed by Facebook to provide images and titles when sharing on social media websites.

15.1.2 Twitter Cards

```
1  <meta name="twitter:card" content="summary" />
2  <meta name="twitter:site" content="@reactjsteacher" />
3  <meta name="twitter:title" content="React.js Tutorials" />
4  <meta name="twitter:description"
5      content="Learn React.js with this Free Course-like
          tutorial website. Nothing but Free Premium-Quality
          tutorials." />
6  <meta name="twitter:image"
7      content="http://www.reactjstutorial.net/react-logo.png" /
          >
```

If you want your tweet to include specific image, title and description when sharing on Twitter, you can use a series of meta tag names developed by Twitter. When a Tweet is posted this information will be automatically scraped from your HTML source code by Twitter.

Twitter will then implement this information in order to construct a better-looking tweet message, using the so-called *Twitter Cards*. Without these meta tags a tweet would simply convert your URL to a clickable link. It is recommended to use this if your content is tailored to being shared on social media.

It is not required to use any of the meta tags. But they certainly help. There are a few other meta tags available in HTML. However, the ones we've talked about in this chapter were carefully chosen for having the greatest practical impact.

16 Thank You

Looks like you've reached the end of this book. Thank you for reading! And please don't forget to send feedback. When a *Learning Curve* receives enough constructive criticism, we make our best to fix issues in the next edition of the book.

Email Address: **hello@learningcurvebook.net**

Learning Curve Books, LLC.

©2018

www.ingramcontent.com/pod-product-compliance
Lightning Source LLC
LaVergne TN
LVHW062315060326
832902LV00013B/2222